AUCTION

FIELD GUIDE

Volume One

Don and R. C. Raycraft

COLLECTOR BOOKS
A Division of Schroeder Publishing Co., Inc.

Front cover (counter clockwise): *1930s Coca-Cola cooler, original condition, $900.00; #42 Super Racer (French), $1,500.00; Grand National game, $200.00 – 250.00; Horse pull toy, $300.00 – 325.00; Summer-Time Tobacco, $100.00 – 150.00; Case cast-iron doorstop, $1,500.00 – 2,000.00; Eclipse Coffee tin, $60.00 – 75.00; Spaceman toy and box, $300.00 – 350.00; Spice tins, $80.00 pair; Transferware ironstone platter, $300.00.*

Back cover (clockwise): *Child's alphabet plate, $100.00 – 135.00; Mickey Mouse toy and box, $300.00 – 400.00; Graniteware coffee pot, $175.00 – 200.00; American mechanical bank, c. 1919, $800.00 – 1,000.00.*

Cover Design: **Beth Summers**
Layout: **Mary Ann Hudson**

COLLECTOR BOOKS
P.O. Box 3009
Paducah, Kentucky 42002-3009

www.collectorbooks.com

The current values in this book should be used only as a guide. They are not intended to set prices, which vary from one section of the country to another. Auction prices, as well as dealer prices, vary greatly and are affected by condition as well as demand. Neither the authors nor the publisher assume responsibility for any losses that might be incurred as a result of consulting this guide.

Searching for a Publisher?

We are always looking for people knowledgeable within their fields. If you feel there is a real need for a book on your collectible subject and have a large comprehensive collection, contact Collector Books.

Proudly printed and bound in the
United States of America

Contents

Acknowledgments

The authors sincerely appreciate the cooperation of the following in putting this complex project together. Without their patience it would never have been completed:

Aumann Auctions of Nokomis, Illinois   Ken & Carllene Elliott
Chris Fricker Auctions of LeRoy, Illinois   Carol Raycraft
Mike Morris   Kurt Schweizer
Lisa Huth   Bud & Sharon Grampp
Randy Kessler   Glenda Bunn
Lori Fricker   Logan Fricker & Woody Hayes
Dale & Vonnie Troyer   Katherine & Elizabeth Raycraft
Michael & Emily Raycroft   Bill Crump
Margo, Nat & Jeff Kier   Capt. Alex Hood
Chuck Conner   Dr. Edgardo Adriano
Tess Bazzani   H. Buster Belmar

*The essence of the antiques business is to take (buy)
things from other people at less than they are worth.*
Chris Huntington, 1973

**The original music on the DVD was performed by
Chicago jazz pianist Jeff Kier.**

Introduction

In the 1950s and 1960s the majority of American antiques were sold at small shops in every city, town, village, crossroads, and hamlet. Many of the antiques emporiums were "general line" shops that sold a plethora of items ranging from door stops to dry sinks and a 100 other categories in between.

At that point it required a checkbook and the ability to carry your purchases out the door. It was hard to make a mistake because containers from England, salt bowls from Tibet, painted chairs from China, cupboards from Chile, weathervanes from Indonesia, and Native American baskets from Taiwan had not entered the market to bring confusion and distrust between seller and buyer.

Today, in addition to the same checkbook and deeper pockets, there is the necessity for knowledge. Many antiques shops have closed, collectibles malls have appeared and disappeared, and the era of the internet auction has blossomed. Hordes of pigs in pokes and birds in bushes have been sold from pictures gleaned from space.

A "good eye" and a bank account built collections that could not be duplicated today at any price. The bank account is still essential, the "good eye" can be rented, but knowledge is an absolute requirement.

Don Raycraft
R.C. Raycraft
www.raycraftsamericana.com

The DVD

Follow father and son team Don and RC Raycraft on their competitive hunt for their next big find.

The second edition of the Raycrafts' bonus DVD is a refreshing source of information on a variety of collecting subjects. The professional dealers interviewed make a living finding, pricing, researching, and selling the items discussed.

The categories covered on this DVD include antique slot machines, vintage globes, cookie jars, Depression glass, Buddy L and Tonka toys, Hossier cabinets, vintage friction toys, and Neff-Moon toy trucks.

The interviews were conducted at the 3rd Sunday Market in Bloomington, Illinois, held six times a year May through October. There were no scripts and the discussions were filmed in "real time" as they took place.

Unless the auction is advertised as an "absolute auction" you usually have to assume that there are reserves in place on some or all of the items to be sold. Rarely, if ever, will the auctioneer announce to the audience that there are reserves. He is not required by law to inform the audience, and usually doesn't.

Generally an announcement of "reserves" tends to quickly dampen the enthusiasm of the crowd because they feel the opportunity for "bargains" has just been taken away. At a catalog auction with the reserves in print the audience arrives knowing in advance the absolute minimum it will cost them for an item. They enter the auction psychologically prepared.

In the 1960s – 1980s period there was almost a fog of despair cast over rural and local auctions when the patrons realized that "dealers" were present. The potential buyers felt they could not compete with the "dealers." The reality should have been more obvious. The "dealers" had to be able to tack on a profit margin on everything they purchased to make it economically viable for them to attend.

The other bidders were not driven by potential profit, but they were very concerned about the "dealers."

Historically, "dealers" have bid for, or accompanied, well-healed collectors to serious urban auction houses to assist in the acquisition of things that would seldom appear in local or rural auctions. These "dealers" (advisors) were present to rent their direction, expertise, advice, and reputations. In that environment there was no reason to fear the presence of "dealers."

In gambling circles, the absolutely worst thing, other than being turned away at the door or dying at the table, that can happen is to be "schniedered." This occurs when an individual leaves the game with nothing or less. To an auction attendee, to be "schniedered" indicates that the bidder has completely struck out and not been able to win a financial duel with the competition.

Both situations create anger, numbness, and a major sense of loss. It is especially difficult because you really haven't lost something you never owned. The auction buff probably suffers the most because of the anticipation that builds several days prior to the event. Unlike gambling, the auction is not an event that can be attended nightly if the fire burns that hot.

When an especially unique piece is sold, it may never be seen again. The individual who has been "schniedered" at the casino or down at the American Legion on Thursday night can blame the luck of the cards. The individual who has been "schniedered" at the auction can only blame himself/herself. The bidding trigger could have been pulled, the check could have been written, and delivery service was probably available.

One of the absolute, basic laws of putting together a quality antiques collection is that the money is always easier to get the than the stuff.

Principals and Agents

The consignor of the merchandise to auction is the principal and the auctioneer is the agent. The agent (auctioneer) works at the pleasure of the principal who officially determines the type of auction and reserves (if any) that will be established, and controls what is offered. If the principal wants something pulled from the auction prior to sale, the piece is removed. In these situations, the auctioneer is the one who usually takes the fall with the bidders. Technically, the matter is out of the hands of the auctioneer and is the responsibility of the seller.

Pre-Estate Auctions

The number of "pre-estate" auctions is growing as couples and individuals decide to dispose of their holdings prior to their demise. As extended care and assisted living facilities increase with a greying population, these auctions produce funds and make the transition from one environment to another simpler.

At many estate and pre-estate auctions, the auctioneer will often announce, prior to the sale, that "interested parties will be bidding." That indicates that heirs, relatives, and extended family are present and will be bidding on some of the items offered that day.

Costs of Doing Business

We will mention, several times, the fees involved in buying antiques and collectibles at auction. Recently an auction gallery listed the following terms:

10% Buyer's premium

All purchases to be paid in full in U.S. funds on day of sale by cash, cashier's check, traveler's checks, Visa, or Mastercard with 3% bank charge, company or personal checks only if accompanied by a bank letter applicable to this sale.

All items sold as is, without guarantees, or warranties.

All descriptions are subject to error.
All announcements day of sale take precedence over any printed matter.
Not responsible for any accidents.
If you were to use a credit card at the auction, you are subject to the 3% surcharge, usually paid by the seller.

Interview with an Auctioneer

The gentleman whose words appear below has some strong feelings about the auction business. He has worked in the Midwest and New England , and now lives in New York state. His special interest is in American furniture, but he has also sold bales of hay, cakes, and depression glass over a forty year career.

"The business is really going to change in the next ten years. It is going to get even more competitive than it is now. I won't be surprised to see auctioneers charging a 25% buyer's premium and not charging the seller at all. If I come upon a good estate with a lot of early things, the seller sometimes wants a guarantee on the contents. To get the business, I have to guarantee them a minimum amount of money. If for some reason the auction doesn't make it to that minimum, I have to pay it out of my pocket. The big auction houses have been doing that for years, but they 're talking millions in guarantees and I'm talking about thousands of dollars.

"Sellers and executors come to me and see what is the best I can do for them and they go to a competitor and see what he can do. I know several auctioneers who have done the "I'll take this one and you take the next one" with their bidding for the estate. To be honest, I have been tempted to do that several times, but it's not really fair to anybody.

"When the seller wants a guarantee, it forces the auctioneer to make sure the minimums are high enough to cover costs, and that's not fair to the bidders. The business has been changed by internet bidding and there are as many bidders online (or on the telephone) as on the floor the day of the sale.The day of the simple country auction, where there are always surprises, is fading into the sunset."

10 Things To Check Before The Auction

1. Before you sign a contract for a sale, make sure you understand it and exactly what is going to take place.

2. Ask people, in advance, about auctioneers in the area. Will they advertise? Do they draw crowds? Have others had a positive experience? Are there "phantom" bidders?

3. Make sure you know exactly when you are going to be paid after the sale. Put it in the contract, and get a cashier's check for the whole amount.

4. If you are going to have reserves, make sure they're realistic. You want to sell the merchandise, otherwise, you would keep it.

5. Compare the list of goods that you start out with to the list of goods on the sale bill. Make sure nothing gets lost or misplaced from the house to the auction site.

6. Pick an appropriate location and time of year to have the sale. September and October are usually not a good time to sell farm equipment and the middle of February in some places can be an issue.

7. Check well in advance with the state associations of auctioneers to see if there have been complaints.

8. Attend one of the auctioneer's sales before you make a decision.

9. Is the quality of the estate or collection worthy of national advertising in collectors' periodicals? Who's going to pay for it?

10. Check on the physical location of the auction. Restrooms? Air conditioning, comfortable seating, food, accommodations, attitude of employees? All of these are critical, and you are probably only going to do this once.

Conclusions:

It is the job of the auctioneer to make it as easy as possible for you to sell and for the buyers to buy.

Think through the process completely before you make a decision. Make the decision intellectually and not emotionally during a very difficult period in your life.

Many times the lawyers know less than you do about the process of the auction.

Work to eliminate last minute surprises.

Be absolutely sure about all fees. Who is paying for what? When? How?

10 Keys to Buying at Auction

1. Drop in for an hour at the auction facility a week or two before "your auction" to watch the procedures, the rhythms of the auctioneer, and speed of the sales. Make sure you leave with an understanding of payment processes.

Do they accept checks?

Do they expect a letter of credit from a bank?

Is there an ATM on the premises?

Can you pay for your purchase immediately after the successful bid?

What is the fee for using a credit card?

Is there a buyer's premium?

2. On the day of your initial visit, or at the preview, carefully tour the facility and learn the location of the water fountains, restrooms, food and drink court, offices, and ATM machines. Also find out about especially good restaurants and cafes in the immediate area. Any motel reservations should be made well in advance.

3. There are knowledgeable collectors, dealers, and "pickers" who can be retained for their objective opinions and accompany you to the preview.

4. After the preview, take your notes, have a cup of Coffee, and discuss concerns, prices, and potential purchases. You don't need an advisor at the auction because all the decisions were discussed and decided before the auction.

5. The " game plan" is critical and was put together intellectually and not emotionally. Stick to it.

6. Do not get caught up in a competitive situation with an egomaniacal jerk who reminds you of yourself. Take all emotion out of the equation. Bid anyway you want as long as you maintain your pre-auction limits.

7. Have a business card printed with your name and cell phone number on it, but not your address. List the type or category of antiques or collectible you are seeking. Hand them out to people you meet at the auction who share your interest and may eventually have something for sale.

8. If "your" item is at $400.00 and the auctioneer is raising in $50.00 increments and your limit is $1,000.00, jump-bid the item to $700.00 and find out who is serious.

9. Subscribe to *Antique Week*, *Maine Antiques Digest*, or the *Newtown Bee* (Conn) and get on the mailing list of auction houses you enjoy.

10. Don't take a price guide or reference book into the auction. All your homework takes place before the event.

Five More:

1. It will be hotter/colder/wetter than you could have imagined. Prepare.

2. Bring a pillow for your chair seat or back. It generally turns into a long day.

3. A candy bar and a bottle of water are usually easier to bring than to buy at the auction.

4. Again, do not exceed your pre-auction limits. They were made outside the emotion of the moment.

5. If you have plans to purchase a piece of furniture, know how you are going to get it home. You are buying it "as is," "where it is," and you have the responsibility to remove it from the premises.

Chris Fricker Auctions

I started going to auctions with my parents as a young boy growing up in Ohio. When I was not involved with sports, following the Ohio State Buckeyes, or reading about sports and the Buckeyes, I was buying and selling items that I found at auctions.

I started working with Eddie Hoffman in Frederick, Maryland, and learned a significant amount about the operation of a quality auction business. Initially, I worked the floor holding up items and looking for bids.

During the filming of "Avalon" in Baltimore, I had the chance to spend time with Barry Levinson, the director. Mr. Levinson gave me the responsibility of finding items to decorate the fronts of the businesses in the movie. After the project was completed, I assisted in the auctioning of the props that were used in the film.

Later I bought signs and thermometers for a series of chain restaurantes with properties across America.

I purchased a copy of the Raycraft's Country Store book in 1987 and was overwhelmed with the Elliott collection pictured in the book. I made it a point to meet Mr. and Mrs. Elliott when I moved back to Illinois. I have since had the privilege to auction off a portion of their nationally known collection.

My initial advertising auction was in 1988 and it continues with two country store auctions each year at my auction house in LeRoy, Illinois. My partner, Bill Bunn, and I moved the operation to LeRoy in 2002. LeRoy, Illinois is midway between Champaign and Bloomington on I-74.

In addition to country store-related antiques and advertising, we specialize in country furniture, Americana, toys, and selected estates.

Chris Fricker Auctions can be contacted at:
www.frickerauctions.com
309-663-5828
LeRoy, Illinois

The Unless You Have a Pony Rule

I am going to reveal to you a basic tenet of a semi-serious collector's philosophy of acquisition. I initially became aware of the "rule" that changed my life while motoring on Route 98 (west) in Southern Alabama. I was on my way to an estate auction in Fairhope.

I stopped at a farmer's market and purchased some locally grown strawberries. On my way back to the car I noticed bales of straw marked for $1.75. I thought that was an excellent buy and contemplated how many I could get into my vehicle. A local whiskerdero with a tattered shirt and matching pants put down a sugar dipped berry and commented, "Unless you got a pony, it's no bargain. And I don't see no pony."

He was very observant. I had no pony. At least not in the car.

At the conclusion of the Fairhope auction, eight ring men hauled a magnificent, "early" walnut wardrobe to the block. It was 10' tall and 7' wide. There was little interest and I intuitively knew that the price was going to be right. Very right. Cheap.

Somewhere within my strawberry bloated stomach, I heard a voice, "Unless you have a pony that needs a coffin, put down your hand, and walk quickly away."

The pony will never know how close he (she or it) came to eternal comfort. Ponies don't care. Buyer's who have to haul the purchase home, will care.

Don Raycraft

Moore's Grocery & The Jingling Sisters

When I was a child in the 1950s, neighborhood grocery stores were a major focus of my youth. Within a six block radius of my house there were four emporiums that sold Bowmen baseball cards, Double Cola, Black Jack Gum, and ice cream cones with the potential for a slip of paper in the bottom that entitled the bearer to a free sample on the next visit.

As a grade school student, the highlight of my day was receiving a nickel from my father on my way out the door each weekday morning. I contemplated through geography, cursive writing practice, and language arts precisely what candy bar I was going to purchase over the lunch break at Snyder's Grocery. A Chicken Dinner, Forever Yours, or Whiz Bar usually was my final choice.

My friend Craig Bazzani and I were under the impression that every school in each of the forty-eight states had laws that made it mandatory for elementary schools to have a grocery store next door or across the street. The store next to my wife's grade school in Southern Illinois was a combination grocery-bait shop.

The high school I attended was within two blocks of another neighborhood grocery run by an elderly man and his wife. The noon hour arrangement in this store was unique because the store offered cold cut sandwiches, Blue Star potato chips, and a soft drink from a cooler filled with ice water. The customer ordered slices of bread and meat, made his own sandwiches, kept track of what he ate, and then reported to the owner who calculated the bill. In retrospect, I would guess that many of us suffered serious short term memory lapses between the last bite and the cash register.

Shortly after my wife and I were married, we moved to a small central Illinois community that contained a barber shop, pool hall, bank, restaurant, and an unkept building that sold "general merchandise." The business had been in operation since the early 1900s and was managed by the two surviving daughters of the original owner. There are probably similar stores in small towns somewhere in America today but this was our only experience. To walk in the front door was to step back in time and observe a store filled with merchandise that had been carefully put on shelves seventy-five years before in anticipation of a quick sale. The ladies who managed the business took their role seriously.

13

They appeared to have no concept that the world had passed them by. They were content to conduct themselves each day in much the same fashion as had their father. The people in the farming community thought little about the store. They didn't think it was especially unusual because it had been on the same corner doing business as usual before the majority of them had been born.

We visited the store many times and tried to buy the spool cabinets, Coffee bins, and advertising signs that covered the walls. We were quietly and firmly told that those things were not for sale.

Only in later years, after the sisters had died and the building was closed, did we realize the significance of what had been there.

The Jingling estate sale was not very well advertised and we, of course, missed it.

Country Store Time Line

1798 Papermaking machine is invented in France.

1809 Nicholas Appert invents a practical and convenient technique for preserving food in glass bottles.

1819 Sir Edward Parry takes tinplate containers filled with meat and vegetables on an Artic expedition.

1820 Oysters and salmon are being sold packed in glass bottles in grocery stores in New York City.

1826 John Horniman invents a labor-saving machine that fills tea bags.

1830 Huntley and Palmer biscuits are sold in tin boxes to English stagecoach passengers.

1856 Gail Borden receives a patent for processing canned milk.

1861 – 64 Civil war soldiers develop a taste for Coffee after drinking daily rations for four years.

1870s Flat pocket tins filled with fine cut tobacco are available on the streets of Chicago.

1878 Chase and Sanborn offers one- and two-pound tins of Coffee to homemakers.

1880 Machine-made folding boxes for cigarettes are produced.

1880s Roasted Coffee is packaged and offered for sale.

1885 Paper bags are commonly being used to package purchases in most American stores.

1890s Tubes filled with toothpaste are being carried home in paper bags.

1898 Vacuum packaging of Coffee tins, which allows long term storage, is patented.

1899 Campbell Soup may be purchased for 10¢ a can.

1901 Lunchbox tobacco containers become available to consumers and remain popular into the 1920s.

1903 Hills Brothers vacuum packs their Coffee in tins.

1906 Food and Drug Administration begins to limit the claims that can be boasted by makers of non-prescription drugs.

1906 Vaccum sealed glass jars with Coffee are offered for sale.

1912 A patent is issued to American Tobacco Company for "roly-poly" tobacco containers.

1914 Chromolithography is developed to change color packaging forever and a "golden age" of advertising packaging begins.

1920s – 30s Peanut butter "pails" are available on grocers' shelves.

1937 Shopping carts are introduced in many grocery stores.

1950s Large supermarkets quickly inaugurate the gradual decline of the corner grocery store.

Timur Coffee tin, $200.00.

Sears-Roebuck & Co, Garland Blend Coffee tin (with lid) $135.00.

Special Combination Coffee from Sears-Roebuck and Co., ten-pound tin, $150.00.

Deerwood Coffee, one-pound tin with paper label, $195.00.

Eclipse Coffee tin, $350.00.

Delicious Brand Coffee, one-pound tin, $100.00.

Golden Wedding Coffee, steel cut, $240.00.

Campbell Brand Coffee, Bloomington, IL., four-pound tin, $150.00.

Folger's Coffee tins (3) with lids, $125.00 (all).

Happy Hour Coffee, steel cut, $200.00.

Red Wolf Coffee, steel cut, one-pound tin, $150.00.

Mammy's Favorite Coffee with bail handle, five-pound tin, $350.00.

McLaughlin's Coffee tins with lids, $225.00 (both).

17

Mount Cross Coffee, $250.00.

Federal Club Coffee, (old stock), full, $100.00.

Advo Gold Medal Coffee from Omaha, Nebraska, $75.00.

Advo Gold Medal Coffee, $75.00.

Silver Buckle Coffee, $60.00.

Yale Brand Coffee from St. Louis, MO, $20.00.

Hoffmann's Coffee, $100.00.

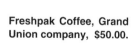

Freshpak Coffee, Grand Union company, $50.00.

Del Monte regular-grind Coffee (old stock), full two-pound tin, $100.00.

Steamboat Coffee, one-pound tin, $100.00.

Manhattan Coffee tin, $200.00.

Royal Jewel, $135.00.

Sally Lee Coffee, $200.00.

Perfect Coffee, $100.00.

Glendora Coffee with bail handle, Warren, PA, $200.00.

Farmers Pride Coffee, steel cut, $150.00.

19

Beech-Nut Coffee, trial size, $75.00.

Atwood's "Private Brand" Coffee, $110.00.

Happy Hour Coffee, three-pound tin, $150.00.

Comrade Coffee, steel cut, $250.00.

Swansdown Coffee, high-grade blend, $200.00.

Planters House Coffee, one-pound tin, $200.00.

Silver Sea Roasted Coffee, one-pound size, $250.00.

Badger Roasted Coffee, high grade, steel cut, one-pound cardboard canister, $300.00.

Old Judge Coffee, one-pound tin, $175.00.

Pal-O-Mine Coffee, with paper label, steel cut, one pound, $150.00.

Pal-O-Mine Coffee with lithographed label, steel cut, one pound, $500.00.

Old Judge Coffee, $100.00.

Turkey Coffee, three-pound tin, $500.00.

Olympian Coffee one-pound tin, $150.00.

Monarch Coffee, one-pound cardboard container, $225.00.

Chocolate Cream Coffee, three-pound tin, $200.00.

Blue Ribbon Coffee, one-pound tin, $90.00.

Fairy Dell Coffee, Peoria, IL, four-pound tin with bail handle, $150.00.

Fairy Dell Coffee, four-pound tin, $175.00.

Wish Bone Combination Coffee, four-pound tin with bail handle, $140.00.

Old Judge Coffee, one-pound tin, $200.00.

Jewel Private Blend, one pound, keywind, $100.00.

Cap Coffee, drip-grind, one pound, keywind, $120.00.

Fairway Coffee, one pound, children on label, keywind, $125.00.

Sun-Kist Coffee, regular grind (old stock), one-pound tin with key, $150.00.

Royal Jewel Coffee, keywind, $100.00.

Troxa Coffee, one pound, key-wind, $85.00.

Jewel Coffee, one pound, key-wind, $90.00.

S & W Coffee, drip grind, one pound, $90.00.

Jewel Jems, full pound (old stock), $100.00.

Stewart's Private Blend Coffee, keywind, $100.00.

Hixson's Coffee, "extra rich", keywind, one pound, $65.00.

Sherman Blend Coffee, one pound (old stock), keywind, $100.00.

Savoy Coffee, one pound (old stock), keywind, $90.00.

Hoffmann's Old Time Blended Coffee, one pound tin, $200.00.

Deerwood Coffee, one pound (old stock), key-wind, $75.00.

Lucky Cup Coffee, one pound, keywind, $75.00.

Red Rose Coffee tins, $100.00 (pair).

Manhattan Coffee, half-pound tin, $35.00; Clover Farm Coffee, one-pound tin, $70.00.

25

Royal Blue Stores, Inc. Coffee, one-pound tin, $75.00.

White Bear Coffee, steel cut, one pound, tin-over-cardboard container, $350.00.

Huntoon Paige Coffee tin from early 1900s, $110.00.

Old Master, one-pound tin, $125.00.

White House Coffee (left), full (old stock), orange tin, rare, $140.00; White House Coffee (blue), more common, $50.00; Union Coffee & Chicory (green), old stock, one-pound tin, $100.00.

French Market tin, Radiant Roast tin, & Golden Wedding tin, $175.00 (lot).

Solitare, High-Park, & Old Master tins, $165.00 (lot).

Campbell Holton & Co. tin, one pound, rare, $200.00.

King Cole Coffee tins, $60.00 (both).

Stop & Shop, Continental, and S and W Coffee tins, $60.00 (all).

Reese, Medaclia D´Oro, & Loving Cup Coffee tins, $20.00 (each).

Hixson's, French Market, & Pascul Coffee tins, $25.00 (each).

Monarch & Fleming's Coffee tins, $20.00 (each).

Old Judge & two Sanka tins, $10.00 (each).

Del Monte Coffee & two varieties of Nash's Coffee, $8.00 (each).

Atwood Flavoring Extracts showcase, c. 1910, oak frame and original glass, $1,500.00.

Bread display case, c.
1910 - 1920, four shelves,
$1,200.00.

National Cash Register, c. early 1900s,
$750.00.

Kraft Cheese display, tin plate, c. 1930,
$125.00.

Oak store display for umbrellas, c. 1920s, $1,600.00.

Melodian player with rolls, c. 1915, $750.00.

"Hot PW Crackers" case, oak, $500.00.

Unusual seed counter with two roll tops over six drawers, iron pulls, $1,800.00.

Scherer four-drawer seed counter, refinished, $1,800.00.

Counter gum display case with reverse etching, c. 1900, $1,000.00.

Spool cabinet, c. 1910, $1,200.00.

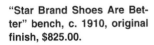

"Star Brand Shoes Are Better" bench, c. 1910, original finish, $825.00.

Tolman spice rolltop tin, picture of hunting dogs, set on counter, $350.00.

Union Brand, LaFayette, Indiana, mustard painted butter churn, $350.00.

Jersey Coffee wooden bin, strong red paint and lettering, c. 1920, $1,900.00.

1900s cast iron Fairbank's store scale, original paint, $500.00.

Merrick's six-cord spool cabinet, circular form with original glass, $400.00.

J & P Coats spool cabinet, four drawers, $800.00.

Roll-top wooden coffee bin with worn lettering, c. 1920, $300.00.

Peerless Dyes wooden roll-top dispenser, $1,500.00.

Triple string holder, cast iron, c. 1920s, $150.00.

1900s six-drawer Clark spool cabinet, $1,250.00.

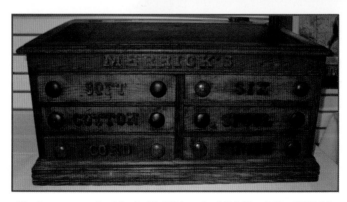

Six-drawer spool cabinet with lift-top desk lid, Merrick's, $500.00.

Six-drawer spool cabinet, original condition, c. 1900, $950.00.

Two-drawer needle cabinet with stenciling, George Clark Co, $225.00.

Milward's two-drawer needle cabinet, $250.00.

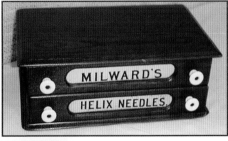

Three-drawer spool/silk cabinet, $275.00.

35

Four-drawer spool cabinet with lift-top desk lid, refinished, $400.00.

Star Brand two-drawer cabinet, Braid Star, $250.00.

Clark's two-drawer spool cabinet, $225.00.

Four-drawer Clark's spool cabinet, original worn condition, $450.00.

Two-drawer Clark's cabinet, $300.00.

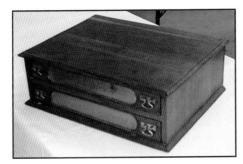

Clark's two-drawer spool cabinet, $225.00.

Two-drawer Clark's cabinet, $275.00.

Three-drawer spool cabinet, $200.00.

R. Ovens Bakery Cakes, paper label, $150.00.

Peet's Cyrstal White with several bars of the original soap contents, paper label, $150.00.

Early wooden box, Soapine, whale on paper label, $150.00.

Oak Leaf Soap, wooden box with paper label, strong graphic, $100.00.

A.B. Bruce Crackers & Biscuits box, paper label, $75.00.

Acorn Soap wooden box, strong paper label of an acorn, $100.00.

Bovinol wooden box, impressed cow, $75.00.

Unusual red painted Kroger box, probably for bread, c. 1920, $200.00.

Capital Coffee wooden box, stenciled front, sides, and top, $1,200.00.

Lautz wooden soap box, $150.00.

Medlar Biscuit box, strong farm scene paper label, $125.00.

Champagne Cigar box, $75.00.

Early Christmas soap & toiletries holiday box, c. 1905, $200.00.

Briggs seed box, counter-top display, good interior and exterior labels, $145.00.

Mother's Oats wooden box with 12 original cardboard boxes, $1,400.00.

Corbin, May & Co., pepper box, strong graphic, $50.00.

Young's Biscuits box with great labels of farm scene, $250.00.

Shredded Wheat box, $50.00.

Grocer's advertising/marketing basket, $100.00.

Croman Bros. counter seed box, graphics, box dividers, $400.00.

Sibley seed box, dividers, inside label, replaced exterior label, $350.00.

Frank Miller's shoe polish box, $175.00.

Hart's seeds wooden, tiered display stand for seed packets, $350.00.

Mason's shoe blacking (polish) box, $200.00.

Challenge Mills spice counter box, $150.00.

Mazda light bulb display, $1,500.00.

Huckleberry Hound Gloves display with gloves & rings, $600.00.

Honest Scrap store tabacco box with big dog and cat label, $2,500.00.

Curtis Penny Candies revolving display, $225.00.

Madame Jean garter display, $100.00.

Dwinell-Wright Co. wooden coffee box, strong labels on both sides, $250.00.

Tin Ex-Lax display with mirror, $200.00.

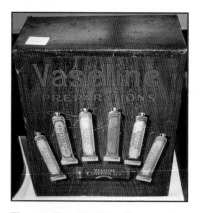

Cardboard fly swatter box with 4 fly swatters, $125.00.

Tin vasoline display with examples, $150.00.

Waldorf pen display on original card, $75.00.

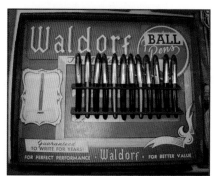

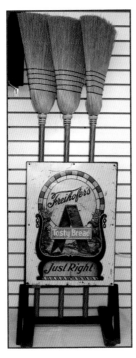

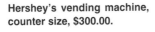

Bread-advertising broom holder, double-sided, $500.00.

Marquette Club Ginger Ale display, die-cut cardboard, c. 1920s, $100.00.

Hershey's vending machine, counter size, $300.00.

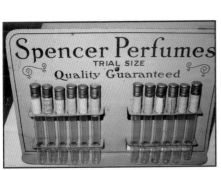

Spencer Perfumes, trial-size bottle display, $100.00.

Peanut vending machine (5¢), counter size, $175.00.

Ronson showcase with pocket knives, $200.00.

Northwestern 1¢ gumball machine, c. 1950, $225.00.

Counter vending machine for cigarettes, $275.00.

Crown 1¢ gumball machine, $225.00.

Zippo revolving display case
with Zippo lighters, $200.00.

Gumball machine (1¢), $150.00.

Northwestern 1¢ gumball machine,
$225.00.

49

Lemon Fruit Drops jar,
St. Louis, MO, $100.00.

Oak trim 1¢ gumball machine, $225.00.

1910 – 1920s candy jar,
$150.00.

1950s Martin's Potato Chips bin with
bags for chips, $125.00.

Glass candy jar with paper
label, $100.00.

Collection of four glass candy jars, $500.00.

Cylindrical 1910 candy jar
with glass stopper, $175.00.

Marathon map display with marathon
logo runner, c. 1950s, $300.00.

51

1950s Kellogg's cereal display, $75.00.

1950s Pasco cleanser display with product, $75.00.

Commercial milk shake mixer, c. 1950, $100.00.

Coast Pack wooden oyster barrel with metal staves, rare, c. 1930, $800.00.

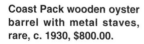

Alka Seltzer display with two bottles of product, $150.00.

Lowney's Cocoa display table, unusual, $275.00.

Jar Ring Boxes

This section is dedicated to the six or seven jar ring box collectors worldwide who live and die for the opportunity to buy original packaging with contents. The holy grail of jar ring boxes is probably the Polar Bear Fruit jar ring box that has sold for as much as $600.00. The example illustrated in this section sold for $500.00. That sale sent tremors through the jar ring collector box fraternity.

Busy Biddy Jar Rings box, $150.00.

53

Web-Foot Fruit Jar Rings, $375.00.

Polar Bear, $500.00.

Happy Home, $50.00; Happy Home, $75.00.

Red Indian Fruit Jar Rubbers box, $200.00.

Sante Fe box, $350.00.

Victor, $75.00;
Security, $25.00.

54

Reliance, $25.00; Reliance, $50.00.

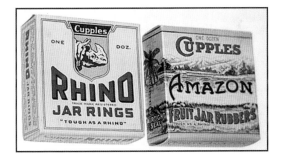

Rhino, $125.00; Amazon, $100.00.

President, $100.00; Beats All, $75.00.

Marco, $75.00; Pheasant, $50.00.

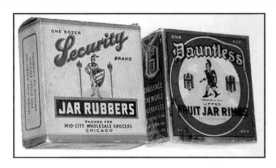

Security, $75.00; Dauntless, $75.00.

Crown, $17.50 (pair).

Shurfine, Best Brand, Excelsior, $75.00 (lot of 3).

Fairmont, Blue Diamond, Statewide ($150.00 lot).

Max-I-Mum, $125.00; Lee, $50.00; Champion, $25.00.

Aurora, $75.00; Diamond Crown and Rex, $50.00 (each).

Grand Prize, Fargo, Our Family Jar Rings, $75.00 (lot).

Good Luck, Lustre (Philadelphia, Pa.) $50.00 both; Pan Tree, $150.00.

Four vintage ink bottles with labels, $300.00 (lot).

Variety of 5 ketchup jars, $100.00 (lot).

1920 – 1940s Heinz jars, $150.00 (lot).

Three early mustard jars, $100.00 (lot).

Heinz Ketchup bottle with strong paper labels, $75.00.

Heinz Horse Radish bottled with contents, $75.00.

Heinz Peanut Butter jar with lid, $50.00.

Heinz Apple Butter jar, $75.00.

Heinz Tomato Juice bottle, $25.00.

Heinz Chili Sauce bottle with stopper, $50.00.

Heinz Sour Spiced Gherkins (pickles), $25.00.

Snider's Old Fashioned Sauce, $25.00.

Snider's Catsup, $25.00.

Superior Pickles, $125.00 (lot).

Snider's Cocktail Sauce jar, strong label, $50.00.

Monarch bottle, $25.00.

Little Sport bottle, Indiana, $25.00.

Buffalo Brand Peanut Butter tin with graphic buffalo, $225.00.

Mosemann's Peanut Butter tin with lid, $250.00.

Pickaninny Brand Peanut Butter tin, picture of African-American girl, lid, $300.00.

Happy Home Peanut Butter with lid, $350.00.

Sunset Peanut Butter with lid, $175.00.

Squirrel Brand Peanut Butter tin, $200.00.

Armour's Veribest Peanut Butter, $275.00.

Teddie Peanut Butter, $250.00.

Montgomery-Ward Triangle Club Peanut Butter tin, $150.00.

Monarch Peanut Butter tin with brownie characters (on back), and lid, $250.00.

Monarch Peanut Butter tin with lion logo and lid, $200.00.

Yorkshire Peanut Butter with lid and pictures of children, $450.00.

63

Frontenac Peanut Butter tin with lid, $75.00.

Toyland Peanut Butter tin, marching band, lid, $275.00.

Red Feather and Bowes Peanut Butter tins, Canadian in origin, with lids, $200.00 (pair).

Oh! Boy Peanut Butter tin with paper label and lid, $100.00.

Kibbe's Peanut Butter tin with lid, $200.00.

Sultana Peanut Butter tins, exceptional condition, $150.00 (pair).

Swift's Peanut Butter tins, smaller without lid, larger with lid, $90.00 (both).

Pair of Miller & Hart Peanut Butter tins, $90.00.

Sunny Boy Peanut Butter tin, $170.00.

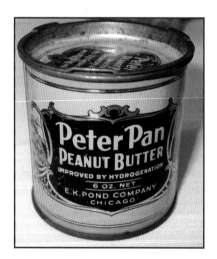

Peter Pan Peanut Butter tin, small size, $95.00.

Derby's Peter Pan Peanut Butter tin, unusual smaller size with lid, $105.00.

Pair of Mongomery-Ward Peanut Butter tins, $100.00.

Six assorted peanut butter tins without lids, $45.00 (each).

Ten-pound Nut House Salted Nuts tin, $150.00 (no lid), $250.00 (w/lid).

Planters Peanuts tin,
10 pounds, $100.00.

Elephant Salted Peanuts,
ten-pound tin without lid,
$75.00.

Evan's Pecan Pralines
tin with lid, $45.00.

Brownie Brand Jumbo
Peanuts tin, $225.00.

Squirrel Brand Salted
Peanuts box, $175.00.

Monarch "Teenie Weenie" Popcorn tin with lid, $300.00.

Full tin of Big Buster Popcorn, marching drummer label, $100.00.

Curtiss Candy Popcorn tin, full, $100.00.

Variety of full popcorn tins; Betty Zane, $70.00; Little Buster, $115.00; RoseKist, $45.00; Princeton Farms, $75.00.

Assorted full popcorn tins, Little Buster, $110.00; MorZip, $70.00; Popeye, $75.00.

Large counter-display-size (for counter in movie theater) of Hale's Midget Popcorn, $50.00.

Three RoseKist Popcorn tins, full, $90.00.

Three full popcorn tins, Gee Gee, $70.00; Jolly Time, $45.00; MorZip tin with corn stalk graphic, $35.00.

Two large (unused) Cretors Popcorn boxes, $35.00 (each).

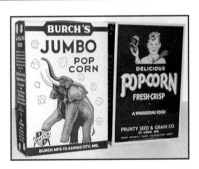

Pair of popcorn boxes, $35.00 (each).

Farmer Boy and Midget Popcorn boxes, $35.00 (each).

Pair of popcorn boxes, $30.00 (each).

Brach's Supreme Marshmallow tin, $150.00.

Liberty Bell Marshmallows tin, rare, $500.00.

Cracker Jack Angelus Marshmallows tin, rare smaller size, $100.00.

Paris' Snow Cap Marshmallows tin, $175.00.

Purity Rolled Oats, $50.00.

N.J.C. Rolled White Oats, $75.00.

Mallory's Rolled Oats, round cardboard container with lid, $75.00.

Jack Sprat Rolled Oats, round cardboard container with lid, $75.00.

Delicious Oats, round cardboard container with lid, $75.00.

ABC Rolled Oats, $75.00.

Four B's Oats canister, $72.00.

Bunny Brand Rolled Oats canister, bunny graphic on both sides, rare, $800.00.

Portage Baking Powder, with lid, $75.00.

Sampson Baking Powder tin, with lid, $125.00.

Musgo Baking Powder tin (full) with lid and dove on label, $75.00.

Soverign Baking Powder tin with lion on label, $85.00.

Vision Baking Powder tin with cherubs on both sides, large, $115.00.

Rough Rider Baking Powder tin with Roosevelt on a horse, $134.00.

Parrot and Monkey Baking Powder tin, full, $150.00;
Vision Baking Powder tin, cherubs on label, $105.00.

Six full Davis Baking Powder
tins, old store stock, $20.00
(each).

Two Calumet Baking Powder tins,
full, Indian label, $30.00 (each).

Sweet Briar Flour box,
strong graphics, $75.00.

HiBrown Devil's Food Powder tin,
with lid, $100.00.

Diamond Butter tin, c. 1912, $85.00.

Diamond Butter tins, cow graphics,
$70.00 (both).

Uncle Ben Molasses tin,
with lid, $70.00.

A & P Sultana Mustard spice tins, $30.00 (each).

Merriam, Collins & Co. staved wooden pepper bucket, old, strong graphic, $180.00.

Bunny Brand spice tin, rare paper label, $275.00.

Christmas candy pail, with lid, $175.00.

Sander's candy pail with strong graphic of children, $100.00.

Bunte Diana candy tin, $50.00.

Three pigs candy tin, $175.00.

Allen Candy Co., cardboard container, from Pontiac, IL, $85.00.

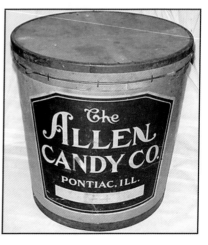

Box filled with 20 packages of 5¢ Metropolitan candy, $4.00 (per package).

Vintage Butterfinger box, $60.00.

Canada Licorice, nine individual boxes, $45.00.

Clark "World's Greatest Candy Bar" box, $48.00.

1940s Milky Way box, $50.00.

79

Ten vintage packages of candy, $14.00 (each).

1950s candy cigar boxes, $15.00 (each).

Holloway's Milk Duds, three counter boxes (old store stock), 5¢ packages, $40.00 (each).

Chicken Dinner Candy Bar box, 5¢ bars, 1940s, $70.00.

1940s Denver Sandwich 5¢ candy bar box, $75.00.

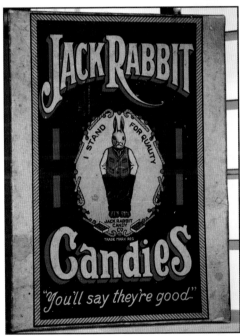

Jack Rabbit Candies box, rare, $250.00.

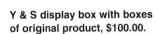

Y & S display box with boxes of original product, $100.00.

Candy Jaw Breaker Pencils, 1¢ each, full box, $70.00.

Jaw Teasers tin with lid, $125.00.

Wrigley's and Adams assorted empty gum boxes, $250.00 (lot).

Liberty Bond Gum box, rare,
$300.00.

Dudley Peppermint Chewing Gum, about 50%
full, $175.00.

Black Jack Gum box, Sears Roebuck, $70.00.

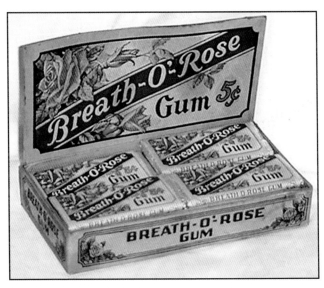

Breath-O'-Rose counter display box, full of packages, rare,
$1,500.00.

83

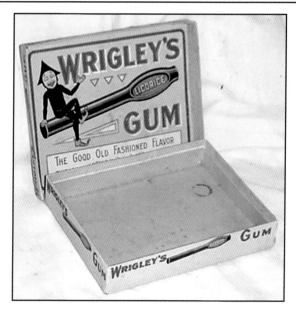

Wrigley's Gum box with interior label, rare, $245.00.

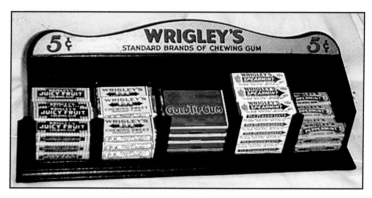

Wrigley's counter display, designed to hold five varieties of product, $275.00.

Assorted gum sticks, including samples, $70.00.

Lot of assorted gum boxes, vintage, average condition, $150.00 (lot).

Beech-Nut Chewing Gum display with original packages, $400.00.

85

Orbit Smart Gum display and packages, $290.00.

Baby Ruth Gum box, 5¢ packages, $65.00.

Wrigley's Doublemint Gum, full vintage box, $145.00.

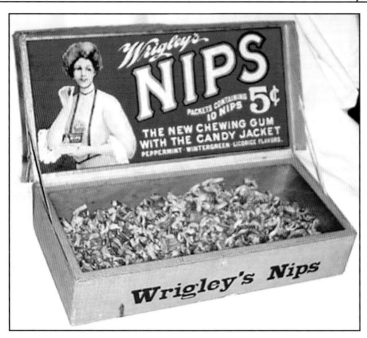

Wrigley's Nips box, rare, $600.00.

Gold Tip Gum, counter display with empty packages, $175.00.

Yucatan Gum, tin display box, $400.00.

Variety of vintage Life Savers, $20.00 (each).

Four vintage Life Savers, $20.00 (each).

Life Savers, glass & tin counter display, $240.00.

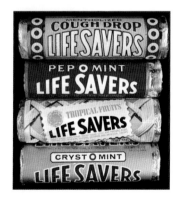

Vintage Life Savers, $20.00 (each).

Life Savers, vintage, $20.00 (each).

Life Savers, vintage, $20.00 (each).

1930s Animal Crackers box, mint condition, $70.00.

1950s Kool-Aid packets display box (full), $150.00.

89

McCormick's Soda's tin, with lid, $225.00.

Pennant Crackers tin, with lid, $50.00.

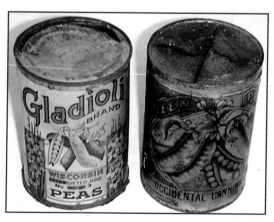

Calumet Potato Chips one-pound tin with lid, $75.00.

Old vegetable tins, c. 1900, with great paper labels, $100.00 (pair).

Old labels on new cans (never used). A can with an "old" label has never been exposed to light or the environment. $90.00 (all).

Old labels on new cans, $90.00 (all).

Early vegetable tins with lids, paper labels show locomotive graphics, $100.00 (both).

Colonial Brand Pork Sausage tin,
$75.00.

Killian Oyster tin, with lid and bail handle,
$275.00.

Brick's Banquet Hall Mince Meat in mustard-painted bucket, $250.00.

Chalk (plaster-of-paris) Chicken of the Sea shelf display, $70.00.

Crosse & Blackwell's Mince Meat bucket, strong paper label, $135.00.

Premium coffee tin with turned wooden pull, c. 1930, $65.00.

Rose Leaf Chewing Tobacco in wooden container, $240.00.

Stud Tobacco display box with 1 one pack, $75.00.

Dill's Tobacco pipe cleaner display, $100.00.

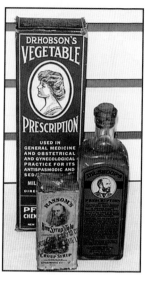

Assorted patented medicines, $50.00.

Ramon's pill jar, with inside label, $205.00.

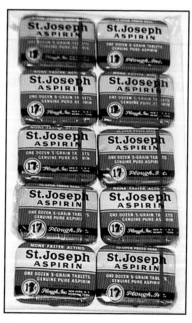

Vintage St. Joseph Aspirin tins (10) with product, $7.50 (each).

Bunte Cough Drop display box, full of boxes, $150.00.

Smith Brothers vintage cough drops (16 boxes), 10¢ size, $5.00 (each).

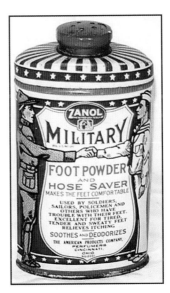

Military talcum tin with soldier graphics, $110.00.

Magic Shaving Powder tins, (full), graphic of straight razors, $55.00 (both).

McConnon Tooth Powder (old stock), 1940s, $70.00 (all).

Violet Sec Talcum tin, $150.00.

Rosebud Talcum tin, young girl label, rare, $500.00.

Orange Blossom and Fairie Queen Talcum Powder tins, $150.00 (pair).

Jaynes and Foley & Co. Perfumed Talcum Powder tins, $350.00 (pair).

Lander Co., Baby Powder container, $400.00.

Pair of talcum powder tins, dancing couple graphic, $100.00 (pair).

LaParot and Fonteel Talc tins, $100.00 (pair).

Kuco Toilet Powder, $175.00.

Nursery Rhyme Talcum Powder tins, strong graphics, $300.00 (all).

Cuticura Talcum tins, $250.00 (all).

99

Violette Exquisite Talcum Powder tin, lovely label, $175.00.

Murray's Lotion, bottle with original box, $25.00.

Sierra Tonic, bottle & box, $50.00.

Old box of gloves, $75.00.

Apple Adjustable Caps, easel-back
cardboard sign, $45.00.

Prudential Sport Coat box, $50.00.

Buster Brown shoes, with boxes, c. 1940, $125.00.

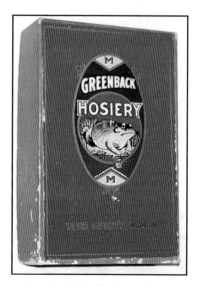

Greenback Hosiery box, $75.00.

Byer Baby Stockings box, $135.00.

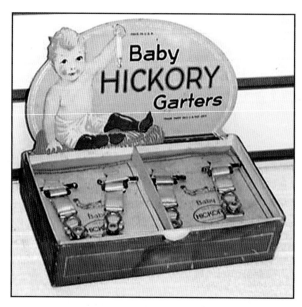

Baby Hickory Garter box, with contents, nice, $150.00.

Bonny's Hug-Me-Tights stocking display, 1940s, ballerina label, $90.00.

Onion Skins and Silk Tissue toilet paper (5 rolls), c. 1915, $38.00 (each).

Fairy Soap display box with 5¢ packaged bars, rare, $285.00.

Sea Side sandpail with eagle and shield, early 1900s, $700.00.

Revere Beach sand pail, flowers and stars, $175.00.

104

Football Collectibles

Game-used jerseys from the National Football League, in the period from 1920 through the 1950s, are extremely difficult to find. The jerseys were used until they were so ragged they were thrown away. Until December 28, 1958, the NFL did not receive the national attention it deserved, and there were very few football collectors.

Late 1890s – 1915 amateur equipment is eagerly sought, but difficult to find. Football vests, leather helmets, and nose guards can easily cost $1,000.00. plus. An A.G. Spalding Brothers vest from the early 1900s recently sold for $1,524.00. at auction. Keep in mind that the vest was an item from a sporting goods catalog and not worn by a specific football hero of the period. If the piece had ties to one of Walter Camp's All-American from 1905, it could easily triple in value.

Early NFL ephemeral (paper) products like programs, yearbooks, ticket stubs, and promotional materials are also rare and expensive.

Unlike baseball immortals (Ruth, Cobb, Gehrig, Cy Young, Mathewson) who left records and averages that can be debated and discussed, football greats like Turk Edwards, Ernie Nevers, Clarke Hinkle, and Tuffy Leemans are almost unknown. An autograph of Shorty Ray, on a 3" x 5" card, is worth much more than a comparable card signed by Babe Ruth.

A wrapper from a pack of 1955 Topps football cards (1¢ pack) and a wrapper from a 5¢ pack of 1955 football cards recently sold for $2,025.00. Both were described as being in "fantastic condition."

If a collector was to uncover a pack or several packs of cards from the 1950s, they are certainly more valuable if left unopened. With unopened packs or boxes of cards there is an air of mystery that you can't put a price on, and the value multiplies.

Wheaties and Post cereals produced football-related packaging that is very collectible, as are broadsides (posters) advertising local or national teams in the 1900 – 1940s.

In the 1958 – 1960 period, Hartland Plastics (Hartland, Wisconsin) made NFL team running backs and linemen figures that were sold at stadiums, dime stores, and variety stores. The rarest is probably of Louisiana State halfback Billy Cannon that was supposedly sold at the LSU bookstore. There were also 18 baseball figures made during the same period which sold for $1.98 to $3.98, depending on where they were offered. The original box and tags are worth almost as much as the figure.

Gridiron Greats

The premier publication for collectors of vintage football memorabilia is *Gridiron Greats*. *Gridiron Greats* is published quarterly by BIGG Publishing, 5082 4th Lane, Vero Beach, Florida 32968. The publication can be reached by email, gridirongreats@aol.com, or by telephone, (772) 563 – 0425. The cover price of the magazine is $8.00. *Gridiron Greats* graciously allowed us to use the following auction results. If a specific auctioneer is not noted, the information was secured via results of eBay Auctions. The auctioned items from auctioneers represent the final hammer price and do not usually include an added buyer's premium.

- Ernie Nevers signed and personalized magazine clipping, Heritage Collectibles, $448.13.
- 1960s Guy Chamberlin signed index card, Heritage Collectibles, $388.38.
- Two University of Michigan Football cabinet photos, Heritage Collectibles, $776.75.
- 1971 Benny Friedman signed letter, on his personal stationery, Heritage Collectibles, $657.25.
- Forrest Gregg Green Bay Packers road jersey, mid-1960s, significant team repairs, signed "Game Worn", MastroNet.com, $8,166.00.
- Chicago Bears vs. Coral Gables Collegians, 1925 Christmas Day program, MastroNet.com, $1,531.00.
- 1951 Bowman Weldon Humble, #1 series, PSA 9 Mint, MastroNet.com, $5,999.00.
- Walter Payton Chicago Bears road jersey, mid 1980s, MastroNet.com, $10,454.00.
- 1922 Dayton Triangles program, excellent condition, $1.626.99.
- 1905 Michigan University postcard with Yost and Capt., Norross, $127.50.
- Minnesota Vikings "Kissing Pair" bobbing heads, NM with original box, $305.00.
- 1965 New York Jets yearbook, 40pp., Namath's rookie year, minor yellowing, $406.55.
- 1933 John Sisk Chicago Bears World Champions 10k gold ring, Robert Edward Auctions, $7,500.00.
- 1935 National Chicle Ed Matesic original artwork, Robert Edward Auctions, $3,500.00.
- 1960s San Francisco 49ers "Flickering Eyes" variety bobbing head, Insidetheparkcollectibles.com, $4,176.00.
- 1960s Houston Oilers "Toes Up" variety bobbing head, Insidetheparkcollectibles.com, $666.00.

- A.G. Spalding Bros. football vest, $1,524.00.
- 1916 Nebraska vs. Notre Dame program, 18pp, scored in pencil, light tears, $2,136.12.
- 1933 Iowa University homecoming football pinback, October 21, $280.00.
- 1925 Red Grange "Captain" football pinback w/ribbon, $569.99
- Washington Red Skins pennant, 29", NM – MT, $384.00.
- New York Titans pennant, 29", NM – MT, $275.00.
- John Elway Stanford University game-used jersey, www.vintageauthentics.com, $3,897.43.
- 1984 John Elway rookie season game-used jersey, www.vintageauthentics.com, $4,450.00.
- 1950 Bread for Health bread label, Y.A. Title, $640.00.
- The Four Horsemen of Notre Dame fountain pen signatures, Layden, Miller, Crowley, and Stuhldreher, www.mgauction.net, $642.50.
- 1924 Michigan vs. Illinois ticket stub, creasing evident, $305.00.
- Baltimore Colts Pennant, red and white, 28", mint, $180.49.
- 1960 NFL World Championship program, Packers vs. Eagles, $301.10 and $434.00.
- 1961 NFL World Championship program, Packers vs. Giants, $53.00.
- Mike Garrett game-used and signed USC Riddell helmet, late 1970s, $405.00.
- 1924 Notre Dame vs. Army program, Polo Grounds, NY, $745.00.
- Super Bowl III media guide, $511.06.
- 1932 Iowa Homecoming Pinback, October 22, 1932, $314.23.
- 1944 NFL World Championship program, Packers vs. Giants, $521.00.
- Don Hutson's "Packers Pladium" drinking glass, $132.50.
- University of Michigan Wolverines game-used helmet, Slater's Americana Auctions, $869.00.
- Portsmouth Spartans vs. Green Bay Packers broadside, Slater's Americana Auctions, $525.00.
- Early 20th Century Reach eight-spoke adult helmet, Slater's Americana Auctions, $1,289.00.
- 1969 Topps Four-In-One insert set w/albums, Slater's Americana Auctions, $528.00.
- Oakland Raiders bobble head doll, 6", "Made in Japan" sticker underside, slick cracking, $405.00.
- Super Bowl IV full, unused ticket, January 11, 1970, Kansas City vs. Minnesota, $831.12
- New York Titans October 28, 1962, AFL program, vs. Chargers, NM, $181.50.

- 1925 Columbia vs. Ohio State program, $510.00.
- 1929 Frankford Yellow Jackets vs. Dayton Triangles, 25 pp program, $495.00.
- Rare 1960s Chicago Bears large promotional bobbing head, Inside the Park Collectibles, $8,500.00.
- 1926 Postcard from *One Minute To Play* starring Red Grange, $89.00.
- 1931 Chicago Cardinals vs. Portsmouth Spartans program, $820.00.
- Exhibit Company archive of 60 original football photos, c. 1950s, MastroNet.com, $29,36.00.
- 1964 – 67 Complete Philadelphia Sets, MastroNet.com, $7,259.00.
- Four 1971 unopened cello packs, GAI graded, MastroNet.com, $2,956.00.
- 1965 Topps Joe Namath RC, SGC 92, MastroNet.com, $2,855.00.
- 1980 Jim Plunkett signed jersey, and sideline cape, MastroNet.com, $3,076.00.
- 1977 Touchdown set completely autographed, MastroNet.com, $2,250.00.
- Johnny Unitas 1956 game-worn jersey, first professional game, Hunt Auctions, $38,000.00.
- Steve VanBuren game-worn jersey, c. 1946 – 52, Hunt Auctions, $20,000.00.
- Football lithographic broadside, c. 1900, 14" x 20", woman holding a melon-shaped football, Hunt Auctions, $525.00.
- Football Stein, c. 1890 – 1900, 7" tall, near mint, Hunt Auctions, $900.00.
- Notre Dame Four Horsemen signed photograph, 10" x 13", Hunt Auctions, $3,800.00.
- 1935 Philadelphia Eagles panoramic photograph, 8" x 27", sepia, Hunt Auctions, $1,300.00.
- 1960s 13.5" L.A. Rams promo bobbing head, Inside The Park Collectibles Auctions, $2,000.00.
- William Hewitt signed check, Albersheim's Auctions, $2,783.00.
- 1967 Oakland Raiders AFL Championship trophy, engraved to coach John Rauch, Lelands.com, $6,693.00.
- 1959 NFL Championship GU football signed by the entire Baltimore Colts team, "Bert Bell Collection, " Lelands.com, $21,006.00.
- 1971 Jim Plunkett College All-Stars Game helmet signed and personalized to "Joel", Lelands.com, $3,478.00.
- 1969 – 70 Gale Sayers GU jersey, Lelands.com, $18,438.00.

- 1948 Bowman set of 108 football cards in Touchdown Football Album, VG – EX, $2,750.00.
- 1893 Univ. of California vs. Leland Stanford Jr. Univ. (now Stanford) program, 36 pp, NM $6,766.00.
- 1933 St. Louis Gunners panorama with 21 fountain pen signatures including Chester Johnson, Grey Flannel Auctions, $1,250.00.
- 1961 New York Titans Bill Mathis game-used road jersey, signed, Grey Flannel Auctions, $6,822.00.
- 1906 (+/ –) J.C. Leyendecker poster, 14" x 22", VG, $282.77.
- 1920 Decatur Staleys 8" x 10" photograph, American Memorabilia Auctions, $1,011.00.
- 1918 University of Michigan vs. Michigan Agricultural College, 40 pp, VG (slight toning), $606.00.
- 1926 Shotwell Candy Company 5¢ wax wrapper, Red Grange, NM, $586.51
- 1921 Notre Dame team photograph with Knute Rockne and Hunk Anderson, 15½" x 11", MastroNet.com, $2,936.00.
- 1959 Topps Cello Box with 36 2nd series packs of 12 cards, GAI certified unopened, MastroNet.com $15,919.00.
- Brian Piccolo signed 8" x 10" photo and separate multi-signed dinner program, MastroNet.com, $1,367.00.
- Nile Kinnick signed page with original mailing envelope, dated 12/13/1939, MastroNet.com, $3,616.00.
- 1960s New York Titans bobbing head; 1960s Oakland Raiders "Toes Up" bobbing head, Inside The Park Collectibles, $2,200.00. $5,188.00.
- 1973 – 75 Los Angeles Rams Road Jersey, Merlin Olsen, MastroNet.com, $4096.00.

John Deere

The absolute holy grail of John Deere antiques and collectibles is the 1837 one-bottom, horsedrawn plow. Its rarity could be compared to discovering one of the Dead Sea Scrolls lining a sock drawer in the master bedroom of a double-wide trailer in Towanda, Illinois.

The Smithsonian has two plows from 1838, but the 1837 version must still be out there somewhere. If you could find a "left-handed" 1837 one-bottom (furrow) plow, you could probably file for early retirement from the carrot cannery.

A critical word amount most Americana collectibles is "surface." A toy (or pine cupboard) is judged, to a great extent, by the quality of its original surface. The closer it is to its original perfection the more value it maintains. If a toy truck from the 1930s has been repaired and repainted, it creates little interest from serious collectors. If it appears in its original box and is found to be in the same condition as it was when it was under the Christmas tree in 1935, a line of buyers with check-books in hand will form to the left.

Most John Deere products that are collected today were utilitarian and in daily use under demanding circumstances. Wrenches had a specific task to perform and suffered from the experience. Today a wrench that has been cleaned, wire brushed, sand blasted or power coated can still hold its value as a collectible.

It is important to note that the "rule of original surface" is often suspended in evaluating or pricing machinery, tools, "oilers," and a myriad of other farm-related collectibles and antiques.

Notes on Collecting John Deere Items

• Collectors focus on specific companies, rather than seeking everything from every manufacturing operation.
• John Deere collectors tend to have an acute awareness of degrees of rarity and value.
• There is a strong geographical prejudice to specific makers. For example, in the heart of the American cornbelt in central Illinois and Iowa, John Deere is a primary focus.
• If a farmer is known to have been a Deere user at harvest, his closing out auction is usually well attended. A never-used tool or boxed part may have significant value to an attendee.

110

• Two-cylinder tractor clubs that share information and trade parts for refurbishing and repairing vintage John Deere tractors from the 1930s – 1940s are increasing in importance and influence. A "general purpose" two-cylinder tractor from 1931 sold new for about $1,000.00 – 1,200.00.

• The John Deere Collector Center in Moline, Illinois, offers a wealth of information, as does johndeerattractions.com.

Cast-iron lid, $40.00.

Repainted cast-iron lid, $40.00.

Polished or brushed lid, $40.00.

Repainted lid, $40.00.

Brushed lid, $40.00.
Note: A cast-iron cover in original condition would show significant use and wear. These were utilitarian and are almost always significantly "cleaned up" before collected or sold. Unlike most American antiques and collectibles, repainting, polishing, or brushing has almost no implication on the price of a cover.

Store display from a John Deere dealership celebrating 100 years of business (1836 – 1936), $500.00.

John Deere dust pan, c. 1950s – 1960s, $45.00.

1940s dealership sign, porcelain, 6' in length, $2,000.00.

1930s dealership sign, porcelain, 9' in length, $3,200.00. *Note: Number of legs on each deer, 30s – 3 legs; 40s – 4 legs.*

John Deere bank, c. 1940s, excellent original condition, $200.00.

1980s advertising electric clock, $200.00.

John Deere 1837 bronze casting, with original box, $2,000.00.

"Right handed" plow, horse drawn, original condition (with lettering), c. 1930s, $250.00.

Stenciled lettering on "right handed" plow.

1920s John Deere wrench, brushed finish, damage to second "E", $35.00.

1920s John Deere tool collection, cast iron, 16 pieces, $500.00 (all).

Wrench collection, $250.00.

John Deere "oilers" or oil cans, variety of time periods, $125.00 (each).

Collection of four John Deere "oilers." $650.00.

Collection of John Deere oil tins, three with original paint and lettering, and one without paint, $600.00.

John Deere girl's bike, $100.00.

John Deere toy tractor (grade 7) with attached "farmer", 1940s, $150.00. *Note: Grade refers to quality of surface.*

John Deere toy tractor (grade 9) with "farmer", and original paint, $200.00.

Note: Original surface on toys is essential in determining value. Machinery and tools can take considerably more hits and use than toys. A repaint could destroy most of any value.

John Deere toy tractor (with box), 40th anniversary Commemorative edition,1980s, $35.00.

John Deere toy tractor from the 1980s, $50.00.

The following toys are from the 1980s and 1990s and have their original boxes.

$150.00.

$200.00.

$300.00.

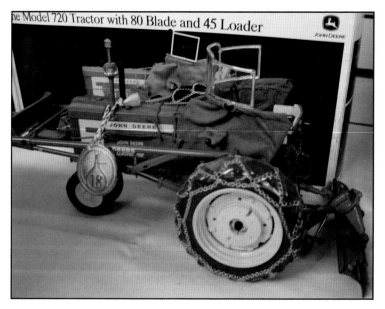

$250.00.

$150.00.

$200.00.

$250.00.

$250.00.

$250.00.

$100.00.

$100.00.

$100.00.

$30.00 (each).

$250.00.

$200.00.

$30.00.

$200.00.

$250.00.

These John Deere toy airplanes date from the 1990s.

$35.00.

$35.00.

$35.00.

$35.00.

$35.00.

1960s pedal tractor, original condition, $300.00.

1980s version of 1939 pedal car, $250.00.

1980s pedal car, $260.00.

Another angle of 1980s pedal car.

1960s pedal tractor, original condition with intact shifter, $350.00.

The shifter adds about $75.00 to this model "10" pedal tractor.

1960s pedal tractor in original condition, $300.00.

Pedal tractor from the 1970s, $275.00.

1980s "4020" pedal tractor, $225.00.

1980s pedal tractor, $250.00.

Tractor with wagon from the 1960s, $275.00.

1960s wagon that attaches to pedal tractor, $50.00.

1980s wagon, $100.00.

133

1940s John Deere dealer's banner, $500.00.

Dealer's banner unfurled.

Introduction of Petroliana

As a ten year old boy in the summer of 1952, I was growing up surrounded by an exceptional collection of petroliana. I have to admit that I was dumb and didn't care. That is not to say that I was uninformed and oblivious. My father owned a garage that sold used cars, and my uncle was the local Cadillac dealer who offered a single car on the showroom floor and provided no service after the sale. There was a gifted mechanic next door (Elmer's Garage) who rented my uncle the space for his dealership ($65.00 per month). The building next to my father's operation on Front Street in Bloomington, Illinois, was an auto parts store that was overflowing with die-cut advertising standups, porcelain signs (ssp), and boxes of obscure attachments for post WWII automobiles. Just east of the parts store was the Central Station for the Bloomington Fire Department overflowing with Old Hickory furniture from Martinsville, Indiana. On moderate days the firemen sat in rustic hickory chairs in front of the station and discussed religion, world peace, tooth decay, and Alan Ladd or Victor Mature who were probably on the silver screen across the alley at the Castle Theater on Washington Street.

With some semi-serious foresight I could have been a wealthy boy if I had squirreled away the Petroliana or the Old Hickory. I did, unconsciously, learn about marketing during that wasted period. My father had a commercial-size mustard jar on his desk that was filled with change. When he stepped out for a moment, I would appropriate a dime (plus 2¢) for an Orange Crush at the bowling alley across the street. As you know already, the 2¢ was for the bottle deposit if I went outside.

The mustard jar contained only pennies, dimes, and half-dollars. One day the printing shop (located one door west) brought my father some business envelopes and a one-page letter. While the man and my father were discussing Senator McCarthy or the St. Louis Browns, I read (as best I could) the letter that would be going into each of the envelopes. I will re-create it for you from memory as follows:

Dear _____,

Recently you purchased an automobile from me and traded in your vehicle. My mechanic does an exhaustive check to see if your automobile needs any repair or refurbishing. In checking under the front seat (driver's side), he found 63¢ in change. I have enclosed that amount

135

and look forward to doing business with you again.

As Ever,

I have thought about that letter from time to time, since 1952, and the one thing that still amazes me is that if you did business with my father two years later and traded in a car, he would coincidently find another 63¢ under the front seat (driver's side). His only child has tried to follow his example of unrepentant honesty and civic pride.

Don Raycraft

Petroliana

The category of Petroliana is a relatively new one for many collectors. The field is broad with gas, oil, automobile, motorcycle, truck, and farm-related advertising and display items as the focus. As is the case with most collecting categories, original condition and packaging are essential to value. It doesn't make any difference if it is a pie safe in Pennsylvania or a Red Crown Gasoline sign in Idaho, surface and color dominate when the final hammer drops.

In the spring of 2005 Aumann Auctions, Inc., sold the Runyon Petroliana and Advertising Collection. It was a seminal event in the history of petroliana and related automotive advertising collecting.

In the description of many of the signs from the Runyon event, the following abbreviations and terms are commonly used:

DSP – double-sided porcelain
PPP – porcelain pump plate
SSP – single-sided porcelain
SST – single-sided tin (metal)

Pectin – a small tin (metal) or porcelain attachment to a larger sign or license plate that screws or bolts on. An example would be the State Farm Mutual Insurance pectin that was affixed or fastened to license plates in the 1940s.

Flange – technically a ridge, collar, or rim that stands out or is raised. For our purposes, an example of a "flange sign" would be the "Men" or "Women" restroom sign that sticks out from the wall in a narrow corridor so it can easily be viewed by someone in need. If the sign was not a flange, it would be flat against the wall and almost impossible to see.

Eldred Motor Oil tin flange sign, 13" x 18", display side rated 6.5 with fading, reverse rated 5. $300.00.

Esso Elephant Kerosene PPP, 24" x 12", rated 9 with a nickel-size chip at lower left corner, sign has some warping, $250.00.

Standard Kerosene Oil porcelain flange sign, 18" x 24", display side rated 8 with overall edge wear and minor chipping in lower field, reverse rated 7.5 with silver dollar-size chip in field and overall edge wear, $800.00.

Standard Elephant Kerosene porcelain flange sign, 18" x 24", both sides rated 8 with nickel- size chips in field and overall edge chipping, good gloss, $150.00.

John Bean Wheel Balance DST sign, 28" x 20", display side rated 8 with minor wear, reverse rated 7.5, $150.00.

Texaco Motor Oil DSP lubster display rack sign with bracket, 5" x 5", display side rated 8.5 with chipping at bottom, reverse rated 7.5 with same, $375.00.

Standard Gasoline & Motor Oil DSP sign, 30", both sided rated 7 with small hole in center and areas of edge chipping, $175.00.

The Kwik-Way System DSP sign, 18" x 36", both sides rated 9, $350.00.

Veedol Motor Oils & Greases DSP sign, 24", both sides rated 6.5 with overall wear and holes at the bottom, $300.00.

Polarine Oils & Greases porcelain flange sign, 15" x 24", display side rated 7.5 with wear and corners rounded off, reverse side rated 7 with heavier wear, $175.00.

140

Shell DSP die cut sign, 48" x 48", both sides rated 9, with several dime-size areas of touch up, $1,200.00.

Wayside Stations DSP die cut sign, 22" x 28", display side rated 7.5 with quarter- and dime-size chips in field, reverse side rated 7, $300.00.

Red Crown Gasoline DSP sign, 30", display side rated 7 with 2 larger areas of touch up, reverse side rated 6 with overall wear, $450.00.

General Petroleum Corporation DSP sign, 30", display side rated 8 with small hole in field, metal loss to one mounting hole, reverse rated 7.5 with dime-size chip in field and edge chips, $1,600.00.

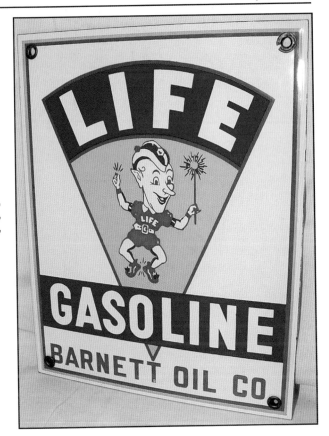

Life Gasoline PPP, 10" x 8", rated 9.75, very nice sign, $2,900.00.

Shell Motor Oil SSP convex triangle sign, 27" x 24", rated 6.5 with large chipping to shell, $150.00.

Cactus Tire Boots & Patches embossed tin sign, 13" x 10", rated 8.5 with minor edge wear, $900.00.

Exide Batteries DST sign, 20" x 26", display side rated 8.5 with minor wear, reverse rated 7.5 with wear and scratches in field, $200.00.

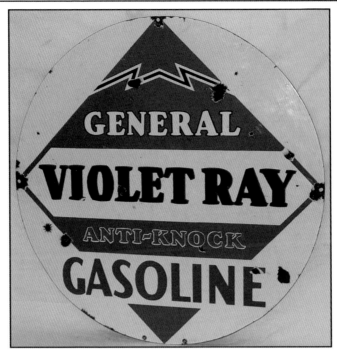

General Violet Ray Gasoline DSP sign, 30", display side rated 7.5 with larger chips in field, reverse side rated 7 with more chipping, $1,300.00.

Philadelphia Battery DSP sign, 18" x 30", display side rated 9 with four eraser-size chips in field, reverse side rated 8.5 with small areas of chipping in field and edge chipping, $1,800.00.

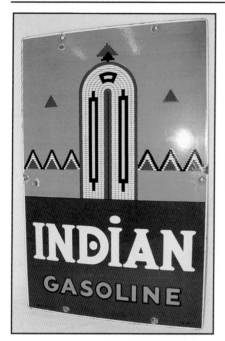

Indian Gasoline PPP, 18" x 12", rated 8.25 with two dime-size chips in field and edge wear, dated 1941, $300.00.

Texas Pacific Gasoline DSP sign, 30", both sides rated 6.5 with two large chips in field and edge damage, $425.00.

CaLso Supreme Gasoline PPP, 14" x 11", rated 9 with one very small chip in field, $600.00.

Tydol Gasoline DSP sign, 42", display side rated 7.75 with one silver dollar-size chip and two nickel-size chips in field with edge wear, reverse side rated 7 with larger chips in field, $400.00.

California Motor Oil Huile Aero porcelain flange sign, 16" x 24", display side rated 8.75 with eraser-size chip in field and edge chipping, reverse rated 8 with larger chip at the bottom, $500.00.

Wm. Penn Motor Oils DSP sign, 20", display side rated 7.5 with two quarter-size chips to field and edge chips, reverse rated 7.5 with half dollar- and dime-size chips in field and edge wear, porcelain has a low gloss, $300.00.

Penetol Motor Oil DSP sign, 36", display side rated 7.25 with numerous areas of chipping and crazing, reverse rated 7.25 with numerous area of chipping, $1,400.00.

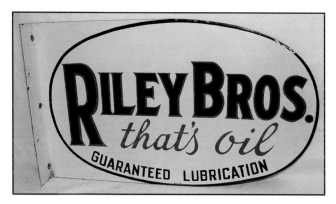

Riley Bros. Oil porcelain flange sign, 12" x 21", display side rated 9, reverse rated 8.5 with minor edge chips, $250.00.

NeverNox Ethyl DSP sign, 30", display side rated 7.75 with
five dime-sized chips in field and west edge, reverse rated
6.5 with four large chips in field and edge wear, $400.00.

Col-Tex Ethyl Gasoline PPP, 10", rated 9 with minor edge
chip at bottom edge, good gloss, $500.00.

Vico Motor Oil Pep 88 Gasoline SSP lubster sign, 10", rated 8 with alligator skin-like texture, $1,500.00.

Autoline Oil DSP lollipop sign with Autoline base, 20" x 30", display side rated 7.5 with overall chipping, reverse rated 6.5 with more chips, $500.00.

Pennzoil Safe Lubrication DSP lollipop sign with Pennzoil base, 24", display side rated 8.5 with one dime size chip to field and edge chips, reverse side rated 8 with more chipping, $1,100.00.

Firestone Tires Auto Supplies DSP die cut lollipop sign with base, display side rated 8.5 with edge chips, reverse rated 7.5 with six-inch scratch in center of field, $900.00.

Gloco Hi'r Octane PPP, 9" x 15", rated 9+, $650.00.

Richmond Piston Rings SST embossed sign, 18" x 12", rated 8.5 with some edge wear, $650.00.

White Star Kerosene porcelain die cut flange, 14" x 18", display side rated 7 with overall chipping, reverse rated 6.5 with heavier chipping, $400.00.

Sinclair H-C Gasoline DSP sign with bracket, 48", both sides rated 8.5 with edge chipping, $600.00.

Woco Pep Motor Fuel DSP sign, 30" x 60", display side rated 8.5 with some areas of touch up on outer edge, reverse rated 8 with touch up and loss of gloss, $1,200.00.

Phillips Motor Oils SSP die cut sign, 16" x 30", rated 9 with dime-size chip at lower right mounting hole, very good gloss, $2,500.00.

The Kwik-Way System DSP sign, $350.00.

Stanocola Polarine Motor Oil porcelain flange sign, 20" x 22", both sides rated 8 with silver dollar-size edge chipping, good gloss, $600.00.

Hi-Speed Gas DSP sign with bracket, 42" x 60", both sides rated 7.25 with overall wear and staining, $1,700.00.

Hi-Speed DSP sign, 42" x 90", mounted on new wood frame, both sides rated 8 with edge chipping, $1,900.00.

Flite Positive Wheel Balancing DST sign, 36" x 30", display side rated 8.5 with overall light wear, reverse rated 6.5 with more wear, $150.00.

Skelly DSP sign, 48" x 48", display rated 7, reverse rated 6.5, $250.00.

Socony DSP shield-shaped sign, both sides rated 8.5, has small retouched areas in field, dated 1934, $1,400.00.

Imperial Garage Automobiles SST embossed sign, 14" x 20", rated 8, has light overall wear, $1,000.00.

159

Amalie DST wall-mounted sign, one side "Racing Oil" other "Motor Oil", both sides rated 8.75, has some wear at bottom, $700.00.

Veedol Motor Oils & Greases DSP tombstone sign, 28" x 22", display side rated 8.5 with one eraser-size chip and slight wear to field, reverse rated 8 with quarter-size chip on left edge and minor wear to field, $550.00.

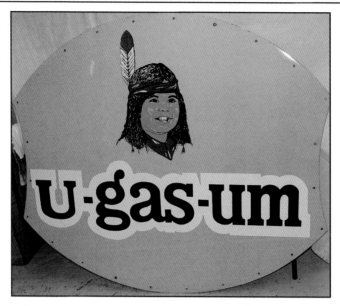

U-Gas-Um SSP die cut sign, 54" x 63", rated 8.5 with several areas of touch up on edges, $1,700.00.

Good Year Tires SSP diamond-shaped sign, rated 8 with large chip at bottom and minor edge chipping, $300.00.

Wides Gas For Less DSP sign, 48", display side rated 7.5 with small chips in field and staining, reverse side rated 7 with heavier chips and staining, $750.00.

Shell DSP die cut sign with bracket and pole, 40" x 42", both sides rated 7.5 with overall chipping and scratches, $700.00.

Veedol Motor Oils DST tombstone sign, 27" x 35", both sides rated 7.75 with overall wear, $450.00.

Socony Motor Oil porcelain curved sign, 15" x 14", rated 8.5 with chipping around three grommet holes, good gloss, $800.00.

163

Caltex Motor Oil porcelain die-cut flange, 34" x 30", display side rated 9+, reverse rated 9 with small scratch in field, $750.00.

Icy–Flo Motor Oil DSP sign with hanging bracket, 24", both sides rated 7 with chipping and staining, $700.00.

Timken Roller Bearing DSP die cut sign, 18" x 40", both sides rated 7.5 with chipping to edges and field, $400.00.

Gillette Tires DST die cut sign, 18" x 36", both sides rated 8.5 with edge wear, dated 1955, $400.00.

Speedwell Motor Oil porcelain flange sign, 16" x 24", display side rated 8.5 with minor wear to field and edge chipping, reverse rated 8 with wear and edge chipping, $1,400.00.

Speedwell Motor Oil SSP convex sign, 15" x 20", rated 8 with two silver dollar-size chips at mounting holes, $450.00.

Ventura Motor Oil porcelain flange sign, 18" x 13", both rated 6.5 with chipping and metal loss at bottom, $600.00.

Price's Motor Oils SSP sign, 21" x 25", rated 7 with half dollar- size chip in field and one touched up area in field, $400.00.

Lion Motor Oil DSP lollipop sign with bracket (no base), 23", display side rated 8.5 with one nickel-size chip in field, reverse rated 8.5 with quarter-size chip in field and light staining, $4,500.00.

Lion DSP sign, 60", both sides rated 8.5 with light overall wear, $1,700.00.

Hood Tires DSP sign, 32" x 36", display side rated 7 with overall chipping and wear, reverse rated 6.5 with overall chipping and staining, $350.00.

Standard Stanocola Gasoline porcelain flange sign, 20" x 22", display side rated 7.25 with overall wear and chipping, reverse side rated 7, $400.00.

Gulf Kerosene PPP, 9" x 11", rated 9 +, $250.00.

Pennsylvania 100% Pure Oil DSP sign, 10" x 12", both sides rated 9 with very minor edge chips, $1,200.00.

Mobilgas PPP, 12" x 12", rated 8.5 with even staining in the field, dated 1947, $350.00.

Mobilgas Special PPP, 12" x 12", rated 8.75 with chipping on lower edges, $375.00.

Choctaw Machinery Sales SSP sign, 10" x 10", rated 9+, $1,000.00.

Wavaho Gasoline SST hand- painted sign, 36" x 36", rated 6 with fading, $100.00.

Texaco Gasoline & Motor Oil DSP sign with bracket, 42", display side rated 8 with some wear, reverse side rated 7.25 with numerous areas of small chipping, $550.00.

Fleet Wing Super Ethyl PPP, 12" x 9", rated 7.5 with hole and half dollar-size chip at top and chipping at grommet holes, $200.00.

Caroil Auto Oil porcelain flange sign, 16" x 24", display side rated 8.5 with minor edge chips, reverse rated 8 with minor edge chips, $275.00.

Caroil Auto Oil porcelain flange sign, 16" x 24", both sides rated 8 with minor edge chips and scratches, flange has bending and porcelain loss, $150.00.

Ospedol Motor Oil porcelain flang sign, 15" x 22", display side rated 8 with several eraser-size chips in field and edge chipping, reverse rated 6.5 with wear in field, $225.00.

Cresyl Regular PPP, 10" x 10", rated 8 with nickel-size chip in upper left corner, $800.00.

175

Texaco Motor Oil SST sign, 18" x 30", rated 8.5 with four small extra holes and minor edge wear, $500.00.

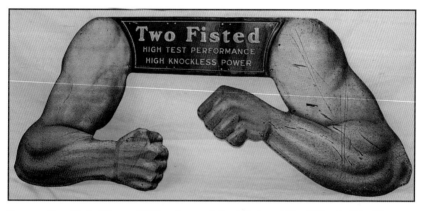

Sunoco Two Fisted Power SST embossed die cut sign, 16" x 39", rated 7 with even, overall wear, $1,200.00.

Dixie McNutt Oil PPP, 9" x 12", rated 8.5 with one dime-size chip at left edge, $1,300.00.

Ramco Motor Overhaul, tin flange sign, 19" x 25", both sides rated 9 with minor scratches and edge wear, $2,100.00.

Western Gasoline DSP sign, 30", display rated 8 with light staining at top and edge chipping, reverse rated 7 with more staining and edge chipping, $700.00.

Aeroshell Lubricating Oil SSP die-cut sign, 20" x 36", rated 9 with minor edge chipping, $3,600.00.

White Star Gasoline DSP sign, 30", display side rated 7 with wear to the field and edge chipping, reverse rated 6.5 with more chipping, $700.00.

Standard Oil Company Elephant Kerosene porcelain flange sign, 18" x 24", display side rated 8.5 with minor crazing and edge chips, reverse rated 8 with more chipping, $550.00.

Red Crown Gasoline porcelain flange sign, 24" x 24", display side rated 8 with crazing and chipping at left side, reverse side rated 7.5 with more crazing and chipping, $800.00.

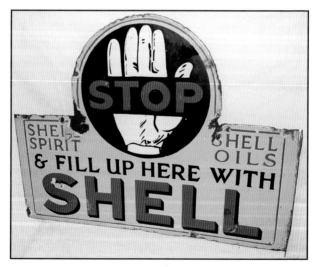

Shell Fill Up Here porcelain flange sign, 18" x 24", display rated 7 with heavy chipping to edges, reverse side rated 6.5 with more chipping and wear, $350.00.

PennField Motor Oil DSP lollipop sign with Quaker petroleum base, 24", both sides rated 9.5, $5,750.00.

Pure Oil Tiolene DSP sign, 26", both sides rated 7.25 with overall wear and chipping, $350.00.

Commonwealth Motor Oils & Gasoline DSP sign, 29"
x 26", both sides have been restored, $850.00.

Champlin Gasoline DSP sign, 30", display side
rated 8 with one half dollar-size and two nickel-
size chips in field and minor edge chipping,
reverse rated 7.25 with more chipping and some
staining, $450.00.

Gold Coin Motor Oils Sweney Gasoline DSP sign, 14" x 19", both sides rated 8.5 with edge wear, $1,100.00.

Jenney Gasoline SSP self-framed sign, 36" x 60", rated 8.5 with two silver dollar-size and one dime-size chips in field and edge chipping, $800.00.

Shell Lubrication Oils SSP sign, 36" x 24", has been restored, $1,400.00.

Standard Polarine Motor Oil DSP sign, 30", display side rated 7.75 with several large chips in field, reverse side rated 6.5 with more chipping and crazing, $350.00.

Premier Polarine Gasoline SSP sign, 30" x 20", rated 6.5 with overall wear and edge chipping, has bending at top of sign, $300.00.

Jenney Solvenoil Motor Oil DSP sign, 41" x 32", display side rated 8.5 with five dime-size chips in field, and edge chipping, reverse side rated 8 with more chipping, $1,000.00.

Richlube All-Weather Motor Oil DST sign, 12" x 16", both sides rated 8 with extra hole in center of sign and overall wear, $550.00.

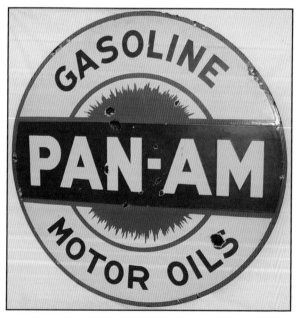

Pan-Am Gasoline & Motor Oils DSP sign, 42", display side rated 7.75 with several chips in field and around outer edge, reverse rated 7 with same, $700.00.

Conoco DSP die cut sign with hanging bracket, 40" x 44", display side rated 8 with numerous areas of small chipping in field, reverse rate 7.75 with larger areas of chipping, $550.00.

Conoco Ethyl Gasoline DSP sign, 30", display side rated 8 with three nickel-size chips in field and edge chipping, reverse side rated 7.25 with same and crazing, $450.00.

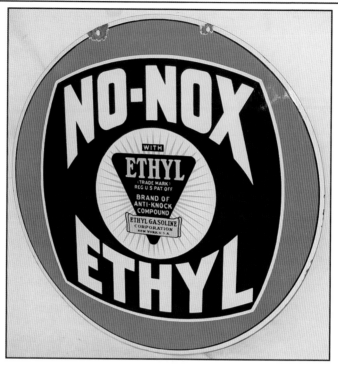

No-Nox Ethyl DSP sign, 30", both sides rated 9 with chips by mounting holes, $1,800.00.

Quaker State DSP tombstone sign, 29" x 27", display side rated 7.5 with chipping and scratches, reverse side rated 7 with same, $200.00.

Phillips 66 DSP shield-shaped sign, 30" x 30", display side rated 7.5 with chipping at mounting holes and top, reverse rated 6.5 with same, $300.00.

Bardahl Frees Valve Lifters SST self-framed embossed sign, 36" x 36", rated 9 with wear at bottom, $400.00.

Liberty Pep Gasoline DSP sign with bracket (no base), 30", display rated 8.5 with two quarter-size chips in field, reverse rated 7.5 with numerous small chips and spotting in field, $1,500.00.

Kurfees Paints DSP display sign with holder, 20" x 30", display side rated 8 with chipping in field, reverse rated 6.5 with numerous areas of chipping in field (has paint can bracket attached), $125.00.

Red Indian Aviation Motor Oil DSP sign, 11" x 14", display side rated 7.5 with chips to outer edge and staining in field, reverse rated 6.5 with same, $700.00.

Vacuum Motor Car Oils porcelain flange sign, 16"x 20", display side rated 8 with edge wear, reverse rated 7.5 with more chipping, $700.00.

191

Alemite Lubrication
for Farm Machinery
tin flange sign, 14"
x 16", both sides
rated 9 very light
wear, $425.00.

Red Rose Gasoline – Motor Oil DSP sign, 42", display side rated 7 with
numerous areas of small chipping in field and heavy chipping at top of
sign, reverse rated 6 with same, $1,000.00.

Eason Gasoline DSP sign, 42", both sides rated 8 with scattered quarter-size chips throughout the sign, $500.00.

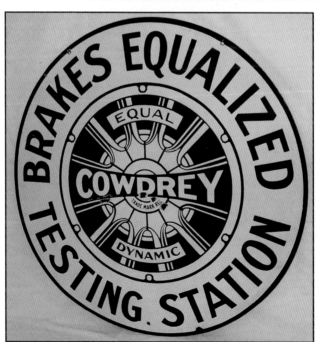

Cowdrey Brakes Equalized Testing Station DSP sign, 36", display side rated 8.25 with five nickel-size chips in the field, reverse side rated 8 with same, $900.00.

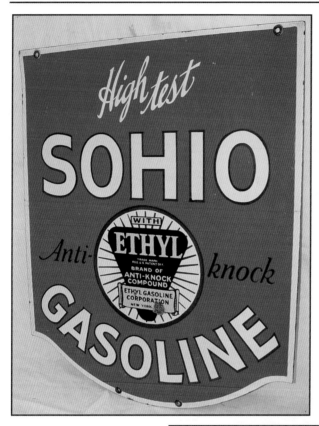

Sohio Ethyl Gasoline DSP sign, 31" x 34", display side rated 8.5 with one quarter-size and one eraser-size chip in field, reverse side rated 7.75 with two quarter-size chips and numerous eraser-size chips in field, great color and gloss, $850.00.

Red Crown Gasoline DSP sign, 30", both sides rated 7.5 with numerous areas of touch up, $550.00.

194

Joy Oil DSP sign, 44" x 28", display rated 8 with scattered chipping to field and edges, reverse rated 7 with same and large area of chipping at top, $350.00.

Gulf Fuel Oil Dealer SSP sign, 36", rated 8.75 with some chipping at mounting holes, $3,000.00.

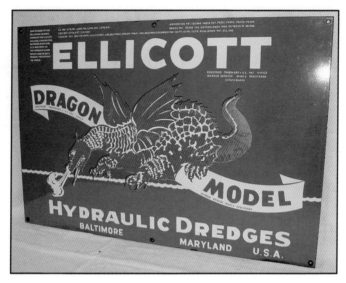

Ellicott Dragon Hydraulic Dredges SSP sign, 24" x 36", rated 9 with some fading to dragon, $1,000.00.

Post Office Lancaster DSP sign, 23" x 24", both sides rated 9 with minor edge chipping, $125.00.

Perfect Circle Power Service tin and wood display rack, 11" x 24" x 12", good condition, $175.00.

Pittsburgh Paints two SSP signs mounted on a flange bracket, signs have never been out of original crate, 28" x 69", both sides rated 9.5, $700.00 (pair).

Burgess Westinghouse Auto Bulbs metal display rack, 12" x 12" x 10", good condition, $350.00.

American Express Money Orders metal and glass reverse-painted back-lit counter display, 11" x 4", good condition, $125.00.

Guide Light Bulbs metal figural display, 52" x 18" x 16", very good condition, $2,250.00.

Pennuernon Window Glass reverse-painted, back-lit tin and glass counter display, 11" x 11" x 4", good condition, $50.00.

U.S. Royals "Replace Unsafe Worn Tires" tin and wood tire advertising display, 11" x 11" x 6", good condition, $1,200.00.

Indian Head Radiator Cement cardboard advertising display with contents, 11" x 11", good condition, $225.00.

Zenith Fuel Filters reverse-painted, back-lit cardboard and glass counter display, 12" x 18" x 8", very good condition, $1,750.00.

Anco Timer for Fords & Fordsons metal easel display rack, 11" x 8", good condition, $500.00.

Apco Horn Buttons for Chevrolet cardboard easel display rack with contents, 11" x 10", good condition, $650.00.

Penn Eaton Motor Oil metal and glass reverse-painted, back-lit counter display, 14" x 22" x 5", fair condition with overall flaking of paint, $400.00.

Schrader Tire Gauge metal figural display rack with contents, 28" x 8", good condition, $2,750.00.

Globe Battery metal and glass reverse-painted, back-lit counter display, 13" x 10" x 5", fair condition, some flaking of paint, $200.00.

Wagner Lockhead Brake Parts metal and glass reverse-painted, back-lit counter display, 11" x 18" x 4", good condition with minor flaking of paint, $175.00.

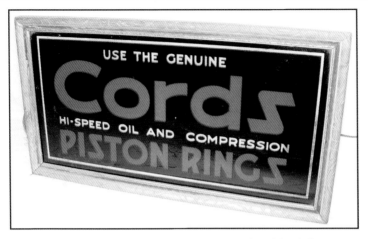

Cords Piston Rings metal and glass reverse-painted, back-lit counter display, 10" x 26" x 6", good condition, $850.00.

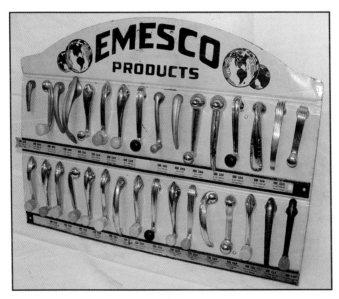

Emesco Products door handles metal display rack with contents, 19" x 26" x 7", good conditon, $700.00.

Mobil Gargoyle Upper Cyclinder Lubricant (with contents) metal and porcelain display rack, 26" x 6", good condition, $1,100.00.

Schrader Tire Gauge metal figural display rack with contents and cardborad sign, 15" x 6", good condition, $1,000.00.

Byron Jackson Pumps SSP sign, 14", rated 8.75 with edge chipping at two o'clock, $125.00.

Tydol metal license plated attachment, 7" x 5", very good condition, $300.00.

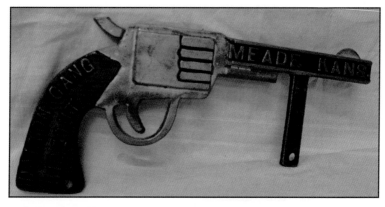

Dalton Gang Hideout aluminum license plate pectin, 4" x 12", $275.00.

Briggs & Stratton Gasoline Engines metal and glass scale thermometer, 14" x 2", good condition, $225.00.

AC Spark Plugs metal display rack with 18 glass jars, 24" x 18" x 3", very good condition, $200.00.

Sinclair SSP self-framed sign, 18" x 117", rated 7.5, has over all wear, $400.00.

Multibestos Brake Service metal and glass neon lit counter display, 8' x 20" x 5", very good condition, $800.00.

McQuay-Norris Piston Rings metal and glass reverse-painted, neon-lit counter display, 12" x 22" x 5", good condition, $850.00.

Victor Gaskets metal and glass reverse-painted, back-lit with neon letters counter display, very good condition, with original shipping crate, $3,500.00.

Hygrade Service Parts for Fuel Pumps metal display rack with contents, 25" x 16" x 10", good condition, $175.00.

Solder Seal Radiator Repair cardboard display with 12 cans, 20" x 14", good condition, $150.00.

Champion Lamp metal display rack with 7 bulbs, 17" x 14" x 6", good condition, $1,800.00.

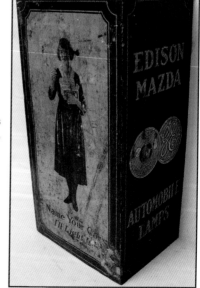

Edison Mazda Automobile Lamps metal display rack, 23" x 19" x 9", good condition, $175.00.

Chryco Power Line Batteries metal display rack with 6 Chryco (6 volt) batteries, 55" x 38" x 10", very good condition, $2,800.00.

Auto-Lite Spark Plugs metal and glass display rack with contents, 20" x 13" x 11", good condition, $425.00.

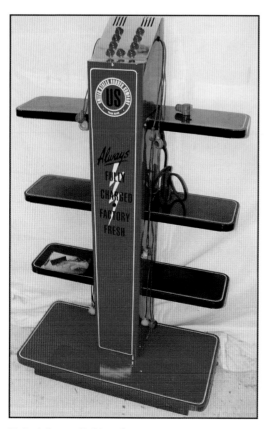

United States Rubber Company metal battery display rack and tester, 48" x 28" x 8", has been restored, $750.00.

Superior Spark Plug Co. SST embossed sign, 18" x 9", rated 7.5 with two extra holes in left side, $175.00.

Allstate wooden spark plug wall display, 12" x 5", good condition, $300.00.

Blue Crown Spark Plugs metal display rack (with mirror), 21" x 11" x 6", fair condition, $275.00.

Champion Spark Plugs metal display rack,
14" x 29" x 10", very good condition, $850.00.

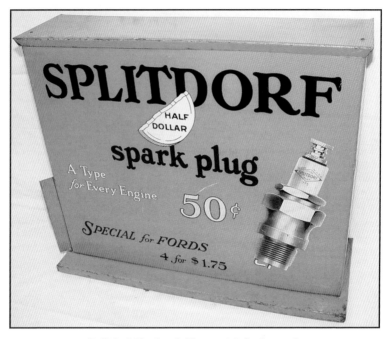

Splitdorf 50¢ Spark Plug metal display rack,
14" x 17" x7", good condition, $700.00.

Tung-Sol Auto Bulbs metal
display rack with contents,
21" x 19" x 9", good condition, $325.00.

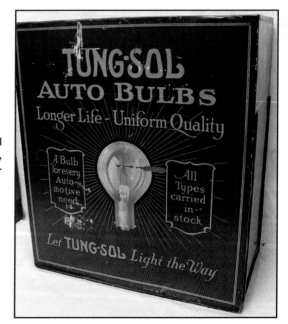

Blue Crown Spark Plugs cardboard box with contents, 3" x 5" x 2", very good condition, $500.00.

Blue Crown Spark Plugs cardboard box with contents, 3" x 7" x 3", fair condition, $125.00.

United Motor Service Genuine AC Fuel Pump Parts metal display rack with contents, 12" x 14" x 6", good condition, $50.00.

Champion Spark Plugs wooden and glass display rack, 20"x 15" x 8", very good condition, $275.00.

Cā Site Motor Tune-Up metal display rack, 27" x 18" x 2", fair condition, $25.00.

Champion Spark Plugs SSP self-framed sign, 14" x 30", rated 7.25 with numerous quarter-size chips to field, $300.00.

Bowes Spark Plug Service DST die cut sign, 14"x 30", both sides rated 8.75 with light overall wear, some original paper still on sign, $850.00.

Gates V-Belt SST & rubber display sign, 57" x 10", rated 8.5 with some wear, $300.00.

Diamond Tires SSP sign, 18" x 58", rated 7.5 with seven silver dollar-size chips in the field and edge chipping, $225.00.

217

American Brakeblok SST chalkboard sign, 24" x 18", rated 7.5 with overall wear, dated 1953, $175.00.

AC Oil Filter SST sign, 14" x 30", rated 7.75 with overall wear and some creasing, dated 1939, $275.00.

Moto-Mower Genuine Parts tin flange sign, 12" x 18", display side rated 7.5 with wear and scratches, reverse rated 6.5 with wear and paint loss to left side, $75.00.

Champion Spark Plugs Service Stock tin flange sign, 12" x 15", display side rated 9 with light overall wear, reverse rated 8 with overall staining, $1,900.00.

Lodge Spark Plugs tin flange sign, 12" x 18", both sides rated 8.5 with paint loss on bottom near flange, $225.00.

Spark Plugs Cleaned AC Method
SST self-framed sign, 18" x 9",
rated 8 with some wear and bending, dated 1945, $175.00.

Auto-Lite Spark Plugs
SST embossed sign, 23" x
11", rated 9, $250.00.

Trojan Gasoline DSP sign, 22" x 28", both sides rated 7.25 with
staining and chipping at mounting holes and edges, $375.00.

Auto-Lite Spark Plugs tin flange sign, 11" x 11", rated 9, $800.00.

Blue Crown Spark Plugs tin flange, 20" x 14", display side rated 8 with edge wear and rust, reverse rated 7 with same, $150.00.

Wynn's Friction Proofing SST die-cut sign, 24" x 20", rated 9, dated 1956, $400.00.

Kendall 2000 Mile Oil SSP die-cut sign, 30" x 20", rated 6.5 with large areas of chipping and crease at top of sign, $325.00.

Veedol porcelain flange sign, 21" x 22", display side rated 8.25 with edge chipping, reverse rated 8.25 with a chip near flange and some staining, $400.00.

Esso porcelain flange sign, 20" x 22", display side rated 8.25 with edge chipping, reverse rated 8 with one nickel-size chip in field and edge chipping, $450.00.

Franklin Motor Cars Service Station SSP sign, 14" x 26", rated 9 with very minor edge wear, made in 1975 for Franklin car club, $325.00.

Duralene Motor Oil DSP sign, 20", both sides rated 6 with heavy overall wear, $175.00.

Delcopenn five-gallon rocker can, both sides rated 7.5, $150.00.

Vacuum Cup Tires DSP die-cut sign, display side rated 7.5 with overall chipping, reverse rated 6.5 with heavier chipping and staining, $400.00.

Jenney Aero, 9" x 12", rated 8 with chipping at mounting holes, $425.00.

Willard Batteries DSP sign, 18" x 18", both sides rated 8 with light overall wear, $375.00.

B.O.C. Horse Brand Kerosene SSP sign, 26" x 18", rated 6.5 with overall wear, $250.00.

Alemite Service DSP die-cut sign, 36" x 33", both sides rated 8 with overall edge chipping, very good gloss, $600.00.

Mona Motor Oil DSP sign, 24" x 40", display side rated 6.5 with numerous large chips, reverse rated 5.5 with heavier chipping and stains, $200.00.

Tiona Oil Co. Tiolene porcelain flange sign, 30" x 18", both sides rated 7 with extra holes and heavy chipping on outer edge, very good gloss, $1,000.00.

En-Ar-Co Motor Oil five-gallon rocker can, both sides rated 8.5, $275.00.

Oilzum half-gallon service can, rated 7, has overall wear, $900.00.

Trico Wiper Blades metal display rack with contents, 9" x 18" x 10", good condition, $500.00.

Hi-Speed Glass-Sparkle Cleaner tin can, 3.25" in diameter, rated 9+, $175.00.

Trico Windshield wiper metal rack, 42" tall, rated 9+, comes with contents, $400.00.

Casper & Oilzum one-quart tin oil cans, rated 9, $250.00 (both).

Socony Kerosene one-gallon embossed tin cans (ten) in metal racks, each 17" tall and in good condition, $800.00.

Shell Oil bottles (tall) in wire rack, all ten in good condition (a couple have chips on rim), $650.00.

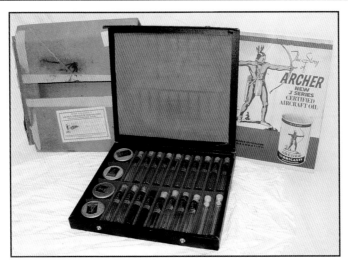

Archer oil sample kit, in very good condition, $175.00.

Solar & Cen-Pen-Co oil sample kits, $100.00 (both).

SOC Credit Cards DS wood die-cut sign, 48" x 24", both sides rated 9, dated 1973, $125.00.

Texaco Restroom Key Holder, rated 8, $275.00.

Assorted one-quart oil cans, tin and fiber, rated 6.5 – 7.5, $50.00 (all).

Assorted one-quart motor oil cans: US Texaco, Sunfleet, Golden Shell, Imperial Ford, & White Rose, rated 7, $25.00 (all).

Assorted one-quart motor oil cans, rated 8, $100.00 (all).

235

Blue Sunoco PPP die-cut sign, 8" x 12", rated 9, $250.00.

Pure "Drive Safely" embossed pectin, $300.00.

Gulf SST die-cut sign, 41" x 45", rated 9.5, $350.00.

Dixcel Gasoline DSP sign, 42", display side rated 8.5 with four dime-size chips in the field and edge chipping, reverse rated 8 with one dime-size chip in the field and heavy edge chipping, $600.00.

Oak Motor Oil DSP sign, 21", display side has been restored, reverse rated 6 with heavy wear, $1,300.00.

Gold Star Pennsylvania DSP sign, 30", both sides rated 7 with overall chipping and wear, $600.00.

Manhattan Gasoline DSP sign, 30", display side rated 8 with silver dollar-size chip at 2 o'clock and edge chipping, reverse rated 7.5 with wear in the field and edge chips, $1,500.00.

Goodyear Service Station SSP sign, 24" x 72", rated 7.5 with overall chipping and wear, $475.00.

Shell Aviation Gasoline SSP sign, 30", rated 6 with numerous areas of touchup, $1,400.00.

Duplex Marine Engine Oil SST sign, 10" x 20", rated 9, $500.00.

Oilzum DSP sign, 28" x 20", both sides rated 7.5 with numerous areas of touch up, $900.00.

Oilzum tin flange sign, 6" x 15", display side rated 8.5 with light wear, reverse rated 7.5 with wear and scratches, $950.00.

Gilmore Oil Company SST sign, 6", rated 8.5 with light wear, $800.00.

KT Oils & Gasoline DST sign, 24" x 38", rated 8.5 with edge chipping and light wear in field, $900.00.

Harris Lubricants SST die-cut sign, 24" x 41", rated 9 with minor wear and bend in lower left corner, dated 1960, $2,200.00.

Firestone SST self-framed sign, 24" x 72", rated 8 with overall wear and bending, $400.00.

Bridgestone DSP die-cut sign, 33" x 27", display side rated 7.75 with overall edge wear, reverse rated 7 with heavier wear, $600.00.

Good Year Tires DSP sign, 12" x 24", display side rated 8 with light chipping and scratches to field, and edge chipping, reverse rated 7.25 with heavier chipping and scratches, $800.00.

Perfect Circle Piston Rings SST self-framed sign, 35" x 30", rated 6 with heavy wear and touch up, $400.00.

Galtex Gasoline & Motor Oil DSP sign, 42", display side rated 8.25 with two half dollar-size chips on outer edge and an eraser-size chip in field, reverse rated 7.75 with more chipping and loss of gloss, $450.00.

Firestone Brake Service porcelain flange sign, 15" x 24", both sides rated 8.75 with minor chips in field and edge wear, $850.00.

Riverside Tires DSP sign, 30", display side rated 7 with wear and fading, reverse rated 6 with more fading, $400.00.

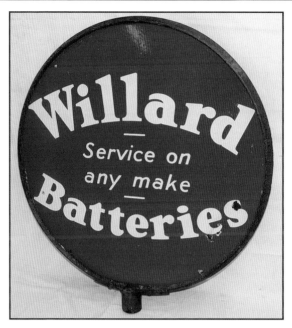

Willard Batteries DSP lollipop sign with bracket, 24",
display rated 8 with two quarter-size chips in field,
reverse rated 7.5 with more chipping, $600.00.

Coryell 70 DSP sign, 42" x 48", display rated 8.5
with quarter-size and dime-size chips in field and
edge chipping, reverse rated 7.5 with several large
chips in field, $225.00.

United States Tires
Sales & Service Depot

United States Tires Sales & Service SST wood-framed sign, 18" x 72", rated 8.5 with light wear, has hand-painted letters, $550.00.

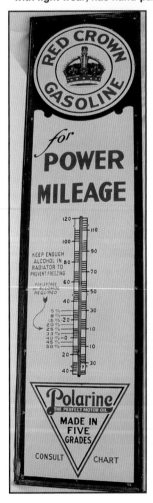

Red Crown Gasoline SSP wood framed thermometer, 72" x 19", rated 8.75 with quarter-size touch up at top left, $2,500.00.

White Rose DSP sign, 50", display side rated 7 with horizontal crease through top and chipping, reverse rated 6.5 with porcelain loss at crease and chipping, $375.00.

Hood Tires SST sign, 28" x 36", rated 7.5 with overall wear, $275.00.

Continental (w/arm & tire) porcelain flange sign, 18" x 22", display side rated 8 with overall even wear, reverse side rated 7.5 with wear and staining, $350.00.

Kelly Springfield Tire & Tubes SST wood-framed sign with hand-painted letters, 17" x 71", rated 8, missing three pieces of frame, $200.00.

Mileage Gasoline SSP sign, 42", rated 7 with overall wear and chipping, $800.00.

Goodrich Tires tin flange sign, 18" x 19", display side rated 7.5 with overall, even wear, reverse side rated 7 with heavier wear, $650.00.

RPM Aviation Oil SSP sign, 48", rated 7.5 with several areas of chipping in field and edge chipping around area of wings, $1,100.00.

Conoco Greasing DST sign, 24" x 38", rated 8 with overall wear, other side is Conoco Bronze Gasoline, rated 5 with heavy wear, $350.00.

251

Bruinoil Bruin Gasoline tin flange sign, 14" x 18", restored, $2,450.00.

Golden Tip Gasoline DSP die-cut sign with hanging bracket, 42" x 84", both sides rated 7.5 with several large chips, $900.00.

US Tires SSP sign, 72" x 18", rated 5 with heavy wear, $175.00.

Brunswick Tires SST wood-framed sign, 78" x 18", rated 7.5 with overall wear and scratches, $400.00.

Cities Service Acme Tires SST vertical embossed sign, 60" x 17", rated 9.5, $1,450.00.

Miller Tires SSP sign, 20" x 72", rated 7.5 with overall chipping and edge wear, $325.00.

Lee Tires SST wood-framed, hand-painted sign, 24" x 72", rated 8.5 with original paint on frame, $450.00.

Firestone Gum-Dipped Tires DSP sign, 20" x 48", both sides rated 5 with heavy wear, $675.00.

Catignani's Ice Cream tin flange sign, 14" x 16", rated 9.5 on both sides, $150.00.

Shell Oil Voltol SSP convex sign, 18" x 24", rated 8.5 with half dollar- size chips around mounting holes, $2,200.00.

White Rose Dealer DSP sign, 36" x 36", both sides rated 8.5 with small chips in field and edge chipping, $375.00.

Freedom Motor Oil DSP sign, 24", both sides rated 8.5 with several dime-size chips in field and minor edge chipping, $1,150.00.

Blangy Time Pieces DSP porcelain flange sign, 14" x 21", rated 8, $250.00.

Red Head Motor Oil SSP die-cut sign, 23" x 31", rated 8.5 with two nickel- sized chips in field and chips around mounting holes, good gloss, $3,250.00.

Zerolene Oils & Grease porcelain flange sign, 20" x 25", restored, $1,600.00.

Calol Zerolene Crankcase Service porcelain flange sign, 24" x 16", has been restored, $4,000.00.

Schettig Bros. Hardware SST sign, 13" x 20", rated 8, $150.00.

Nourse "Business Is Good" DSP sign, 28", display side has been restored, reverse side rated 5, $1,100.00.

Musgo Gasoline DSP sign, 48", display side rated 7 with several large touched up areas, (no chipping to the face and headdress area of the Indian), reverse side rated 3, $5,250.00.

Union 76 Certified Car Condition Service SSP sign, 22", rated 9+, $1,000.00.

AOAA Blue List Travel Service DSP die-cut sign, 20" x 18", both sides rated 8, $775.00.

Consolidated Tous DSP die-cut sign, 19" x 22", display rated 8.5, reverse rated 7 has crazing and chips at bottom, $500.00.

Sea Sled Boats SST sign, 15" x 28", rated 8 with overall even wear, $350.00.

Continental Red Seal Air-Cooled Engines reverse-painted on glass, 8" x 16", rated 9, $250.00.

Mack Building Plaque, $75.00.

Liberty Trucking Co. tin thermometer and calendar holder, 16" x 8", rated 8, $100.00.

Polarine for "F" Fords half-gallon flat tin can, rated 9+, $425.00.

Texaco flat half-gallon swing spout tin can, rated 9, $575.00.

Prestone Anti-Freeze round porcelain thermometer, 10", rated 7.5, has chips and glass is cracked, $150.00.

Red Seal Dry Battery porcelain thermometer, 27" x 7", rated 8.5, has chips around both mounting holes, $550.00.

Sterling Motor Oils DST paddle sign, 6", rated 9 with paper marks, $225.00.

Water Tower, spring in middle has been repainted, $300.00.

Prestone Anti-Freeze porcelain die-cut thermometer 36" x 9", rated 7.5 with edge chipping, good gloss, $150.00.

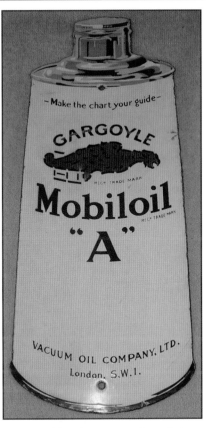

Mobiloil SSP die-cut can- shaped sign, 19" x 7", rated 7.5, overall wear and roughness around edges, $1,150.00.

Pure Premium & Pure-Pep PPP's, 12" x 10", rated 9+, $275.00 (both).

Hart Batteries SSP convex sign, 9" x 24", rated 9+, has excellent gloss, $1,700.00.

Oliver C. Steele Mfg. Co. of Spiceland, IN "Duck Shades" neon salesman's portable display in steel carrying case (with front cover), 12" x 24", rated 9, $950.00.

Good Year Tires SSP sign, 35" x 94", rated 7.5 with overall chipping and edge wear, $375.00.

Texaco Sky Chief PPP, 18" x 12", rated 8 with some chipping at grommet holes, dated 1959, $200.00.

Standard Motor Gasoline SSP pricer sign, 48" x 18", has been restored, $1,700.00.

Red Crown Gasoline SST sign, 19" x 14", rated 6 with overall heavy wear, $200.00.

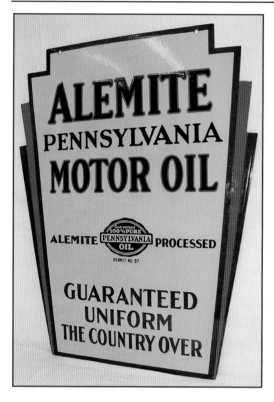

Alemite Motor Oil DSP die-cut sign, 30" x 24", has been restored, $1,100.00.

Hi-Line Montana Made Gasoline DSP sign, 30", display side has been restored, reverse side rated 5, $550.00.

Dodgem Bumper Car, 66" long, has been converted to gasoline motor (4 cycle), good condition, $1,600.00.

Gulf Refining Supreme Auto Oil porcelain flange sign, 11" x 15", both sides rated 9, porcelain has low gloss, $1,300.00.

Weed Tire Chains SST wood-framed calculator sign, rated 9 with minor edge wear, $2,750.00.

Atlantic Stop-Wear Service SSP sign, 24", rated 7 with quarter-size chip in field and heavy edge chipping, $325.00.

Motorite Motor Oil die-cut flange sign, 20" x 19", display side rated 8 with silver dollar-size chip at top and minor edge chipping, reverse rated 7.5 with larger chipping at top, $800.00.

Standard Gasoline Pinocchio SST sign, 24", restored, $3,500.00.

RPM Motor Oil SST sign, 24", has been restored, $1,600.00.

Zerolene Lubrication SSP sign, 15" x 20", restored, $600.00.

Zerolene DSP sign, 27" x 27", both sides have been restored, $600.00.

Richfield SSP die-cut sign, 27" x 35", has been restored, $500.00.

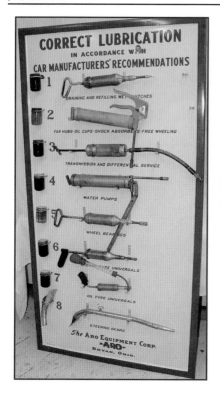

Aro Equipment Co. SSP display rack with contents, 66" x 35", rated 9 with quarter-size chip in top area, $1,000.00.

Caltex Kerosene SSP sign, 24" x 36", rated 7 with chipping and touch up to edges, $375.00.

Standard Stanocola SSP sign, 30", restored, $2,000.00.

Standard Oil Stanocola SSP sign, 18", restored, $1,200.00.

Shell Premium Gasoline shell-shaped PPP, 12" x 12", restored, $700.00.

Staroleum Motor Oil, SSP sign, 30", restored, $500.00.

Standard Oil Stanocola Polarine SSP sign, 18" x 36", restored, $1,000.00.

Texaco Motor Oil DSP curb sign with Texaco base, 30" x 30", display side rated 7.5 with large chips in field, reverse side rated 7 with more chipping, $300.00.

Good Year Service Station two-piece SST wood-framed sign, 27" x 48", rated 6 with overall wear and some rust, $450.00.

Dauchy's Auto Motor Oil tin flange sign, 7" x 18", both sides rated 7.5 with overall, even wear, $350.00.

Pennzoil Safe Lubrication SSP sign, 15" x 27", rated 8 with several areas of touch up to the edges, $475.00.

Headlight Overalls SSP sign, 10" x 32", has been restored, $550.00.

HyVis Motor Oil DSP sign, 17" x 26", display side rated 8 with chipping at the mounting holes and edges, reverse side rated 7.5 with more chipping, $500.00.

White House Motor Oil SSP self-framed sign, 19" x 25", rated 8.5 with nickel-size chip in field and extra-small hole at bottom with edge chipping, $700.00.

Better Gasoline & Oils DSP sign, 36", display side rated 8 with scratches to the field and edge chipping, reverse rated 7 with more wear, $550.00

Exide Batteries tin flange die-cut sign, 14" x 14", both sides rated 8.5 with some light wear, $550.00.

Amoco DSP sign, 48" x 72", display side rated 8.5 with several small chips in field, reverse side rated 8 with more chipping and stains, $350.00.

Good Year Tires DSP sign, 27" x 48", both sides rated 7.5 with wear in field and chipping at mounting holes and edges, $400.00

Pierce Oil SSP convex sign, 15", restored, $800.00.

Linco Motor Oils DSP sign, 30", both sides rated poor, $150.00.

Sternol Oil & Greases porcelain flange sign, 18" x 21", rated 8 with edge chipping and minor field wear, $100.00.

Delco America's No. 1 Battery DST die-cut sign, 17" x 33", display rated 8 with edge wear, reverse side rated 7 with edge wear and staining in field, $350.00.

Continental Tires DSP sign, 13" x 22", display side has been restored, reverse rated poor, $550.00.

Goodrich Tires Garage porcelain flange sign, 14" x 18", display side rated 8.25 with scratches in field and edge chips, reverse 7 with half-dollar-size chip in field and overall wear, $300.00.

Standard Motor Oil SSP sign, 18" x 36", rated 7 with several area of large chipping and edge wear, $150.00.

Willard Storage Battery Service Station DSP sign, 15" x 24", display side rated 7.5 with edge chipping and staining, reverse rated 6.5 with larger area of chipping, $175.00.

Penno "Unexcelled" Motor Oil tin flange sign, 13" x 18", both sides rated 9+, $800.00.

RPM Motor Oil DSP sign, 30", both sides rated 8.5 with edge chipping, $400.00.

American Gasoline PPP, 12", has been restored, $700.00.

India Tires SSP sign, 18" x 60", rated 8.5 with some color fading, $600.00.

Federal Lubricants SSP sign, 10" x 20", rated 7.5 with overall wear, $75.00.

India Tire SSP sign, 24" x 72", rated 9 with minor chips at two grommet holes, $450.00.

Welch-Penn Motor Oil SST sign, 9" x 24", rated 9 with light overall wear, $325.00.

Welch Motor Oil SST sign, 9" x 24", rated 9 with light overall wear, $375.00.

Firestone Tires porcelain flange sign, 16" x 21", display side rated 8 with edge chips and wear in field, reverse side rated 7.5, $200.00.

D-X Motor Oil DSP sign, 20" x 30", display side rated 9, reverse rated 8.5 with chipping on lower edge and scratches, $375.00.

Powerine Gas DSP sign, 20" x 28", display side rated 6.5 with overall chipping and wear, reverse side rated 6, $150.00.

Kendall Pennzbest Motor Oils porcelain flange sign, 12" x 12", display side rated 8 with silver dollar-size chip on lower edge, reverse side rated 7.5 with chipping on bottom, $300.00.

Dixie Ethyl PPP 12", restored, $800.00.

Champion Spark Plugs tin flange sign, 12" x 18", both sides rated 9, still has some paper on flange, $250.00.

Pennsylvania Tires DST keystone-shaped sign, 36" x 32", both sides rated 7.5 with overall wear, $50.00.

Amoco American Gas DSP sign, 54" x 96", display side rated 7.5 with scattered chipping, reverse side rated 6.5, $325.00.

Beacon Penn Motor Oil DSP sign, 30" x 30", both sides rated 6.5 with large areas of chipping and overall wear, $275.00.

Stoll Golden-Tip Gasoline SSP sign, 36" x 48", rated 6.5, with several areas of touch up and wear, $300.00.

Diamond Tires DST sign, 26" x 42", both sides rated 8 with overall wear, dated 1939, $275.00.

Trojan Batteries SST die-cut sign, 38" x 45", rated 9 with scratch in field, $657.00.

Lubri-Loy Oil SST embossed, can-shaped sign, 58" x 36", rated 8 with overall wear, $500.00.

Wizard Gasoline Tonic tin flange sign, 15" x 18", both sides rated 8 with overall wear, $225.00.

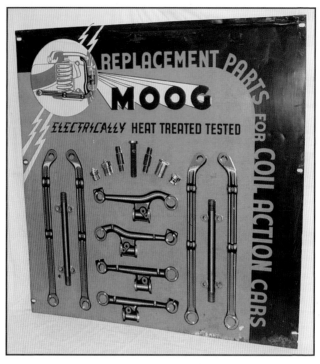

Moog Replacement Parts SST embossed sign, 39" x 39", rated 8 with overall edge wear, $500.00.

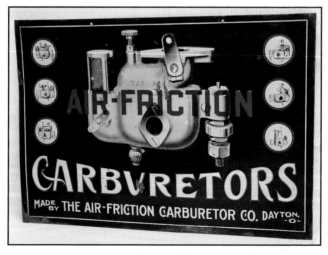

Air-Friction Carburetors SST embossed sign, 13" x 20", rated 7.5 with two small holes in field and overall wear, $300.00.

Ajax Antifreeze SST wood-framed thermometer, 36" x 24", rated 7.5 with wear and spotting, $400.00.

Airco Products SSP sign, 35" x 30", rated 8 with quarter-size chip in field and chips at mounting holes, $225.00.

Young's Choice Kerosene tin flange sign, 12" x 16", both sides rated 8.5 with light wear, $150.00.

Empire Tires tin flange sign, 12" x 18", display side rated 7 with wear and rust, reverse rated 6.5 with wear, $175.00.

American DSP sign, 45" x 75", both sides rated 8.25 with chipping at top , dated 1964, $275.00.

Compensating Vapor Plug tin-over-cardboard sign, 11" x 16", rated 9, $525.00.

Goodrich Silvertowns porcelain flange sign, 19" x 23", display side rated 8 with several chips in field and on edges, reverse rated 7 with heavier chipping and crazing, $200.00.

Ethyl PPP, 8", rated 9 with minor edge wear, $100.00.

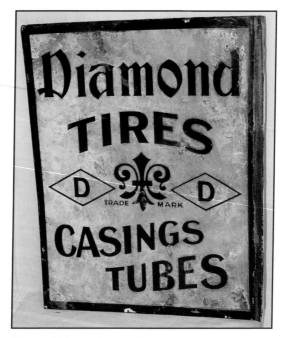

Diamond Tires porcelain flange sign, 17" x 13", both
sides rated 5.5 with heavy wear, $275.00.

Pedrick Piston Ring Service DST sign, 20" x 28", rated 9 with light wear, $350.00.

Sterling Ethyl Gasoline DSP sign, 30", display side rated 9 with
one dime-size chip below logo, reverse side rated 8.5 with quarter-size and eraser-size chips in field, $1,450.00.

Notes on Collecting Soft-Drink-Related Memorabilia

- 1. The vast majority of collectors accumulate the wares of national makers (Pepsi-Cola, Coca-Cola).
- 2. There are more Coca-Cola collectors than Pepsi but there are also considerably more Coca-Cola items to find. Both are very serious categories of soda collecting.
- 3. Regional drinks (Moxie, Alex) have collectors who tend to be from the geographic area where the drink is (was) featured. Ale8 material is more valuable in Lexington, Kentucky and the immediate vicinity than anywhere else on earth.
- 4. There are a minimum 1,500 different local soft drink brands that were popular somewhere for short periods in cities, towns, and American Legion outposts in the 1946 – early-1960s era. Eventually most could not compete with the national brands and went out of business.
- 5. Local soft drink signs and products from the 1940s to 1960s are presently underpriced in the world of soda-pop collecting.
- 6. Six absolute keys (and 1 bonus) to determining value:

   a. **surface:** This is critical to the value of any antique or collectible, except to buyers of vintage John Deere tractors. They expect the tractor to be in worn condition and the repainting process is automatic. It doesn't make any difference if it's a Pepsi-Cola bottle with a paper label or a Pez dispenser, it all comes down to surface and the degree of the original condition.

   b. **condition:** In evaluating porcelain signs and advertising, many auctioneers use a 1-10 rating scale so there is a kind of semi-universal understanding, but 8.5 in Peoria is not necessarily 8.5 in Indianapolis. As we have noted previously, a truly great piece can take a bigger condition hit than a relatively common example, but condition is equally as important as surface. Mechanical restoration is almost always a positive step for value because it is not evident on the surface of the piece.

   c. **age:** Soda-pop memorabilia from the late nineteenth century-early 1900s is extremely rare. Items from the 1915 to 1930s period are more frequently found, but are still very rare. Almost anything from the 1940s to 1950s could be approaching the "uncommon, but still out there" region.

   d. **color:** Some products were made for brief periods in colors that add significantly to the value of a piece.

e. **degree of rarity:** Value can turn on an extra dot in the right place. Serious collectors are serious because they know and recognize the variations.

f. **type of collectible:** All makers did not produce equal numbers of a given product. Porcelain signs are (usually) rarer than comparable tin (plate) examples. If a soft-drink cooler or coin-operated machine (pop) has been repainted, or had the surface enhanced, or altered (new decal's), the value is seriously compromised. Expect wear and look for it. Very few machines were not kicked, cursed, hit, scratched, or dented somewhere. Thirsty customers on hot days tend to over react when things go awry.

g. **(bonus) warehouse finds:** Periodically, a box of signs from the 1930s is uncovered in the basement of a storefront under going demolition or reconstruction. These signs are usually pristine. Initially, prices are high because most collectors have never seen them. The key is how they are released into the marketplace. If they come out one or two at a time over a wide geographic area, the initial price can even increase. If 1,000 show up, the price structure will suffer. Thirty years down the road, after being absorbed into collections, they become legitimately rare again.

1940s two-sided "light pulls," $75.00 (all).

1930s Coca-Cola cooler, original condition, $900.00.

Side view of cooler above.

Similar cooler from the 1930s that received more use, $350.00.

Close up of trademark.

1950s – '60s Coke machine, $1,000.00.

1960s display sign, $150.00.

1960s tin (plate) sign, $600.00.

Coca-Cola 5¢ machine from early 1950s, $1,200.00.

Unusual bottle display with painted bottle, $100.00.

Late 1960s tin (plate) sign, $150.00.

"Safety First" sidewalk marker, heavily reproduced, $50.00.

Coke machine, c. 1940s, $1,700.00.

"Drink Coca-Cola" sign, 1960s, $180.00.

1940s tin (plate) sign, $175.00.

1940s flange sign, $500.00.

1950s "fish tail" sign, $1,400.00.

1950s cardboard restaurant sign, $75.00.

1950s "fish tail" sign, $350.00.

1940s grocery bag holder, $800.00.

1960s tin (plate) "fish tail" sign, $260.00.

Late-1960s tin (plate) sign, $135.00.

309

Porcelain sign (two-sided), $1,200.00.

Porcelain "button" sign, 48", $500.00.

1950s flange sign, $450.00.

Small plastic chest, $200.00.

Porcelain "button" sign, 48", $400.00.

Porcelain "button" sign, 48", $400.00.

Radio designed to look like a cooler, rare, $1,000.00.

Wood-framed, cardboard sign featuring the Harlem Globetrotters, unusual and rare, $750.00.

313

1950s calendar holder, $225.00.

Thermometers, at left $210.00; at right $260.00.

Menu board, $400.00.

1960s carrier (tin) with six bottles, $105.00.

1970s two-bottle card-
board carrier, $25.00.

1940s cardboard six-pack carrier, $75.00.

Canvas bottle carrier, $105.00.

1960s heavy cardboard carrier, $80.00.

Child's toy dispenser with cups, $80.00.

1960s cardboard picnic scene, $150.00.

1950s hanging "fish tail" restaurant light, $525.00.

1940s store window display for "Fruits & 7Up", $130.00.

1960 tin (plate) sign, $165.00.

1960s Chevron sign, $150.00.

1970s tin (plate) sign, $100.00.

1960s Coca-Cola cardboard sign with "danglers", $160.00.

1930s porcelain "brick" sign, $385.00.

1960s Dr Pepper Chevron display-rack sign, $125.00.

1960s cash register "light up", $155.00. Note: "Light ups" were used at cash registers to attract the customer's attention for marketing purposes.

1950s driver's hat from 7UP, $80.00.

1960s cardboard restaurant sign, $140.00.

Late-1960s psychedelic "light up", $275.00.

1940s tin (plate) embossed Orange Crush sign, $250.00.

1960s celluloid button with envelope, $125.00.

1930s Orange-Crush sign (tin), $375.00.

1970s Squirt menu board from a restaurant, $80.00.

1960s Squirt sign, tin (plate), $240.00.

1960s Squirt sign, $265.00.

1970s tin (plate) embossed sign, $100.00.

Mountain Dew sign, embossed tin (plate), $925.00.

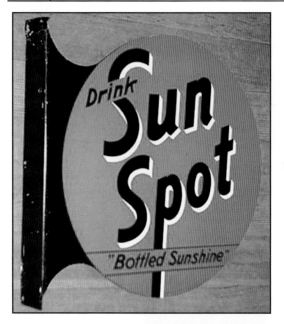

1950s Sun Spot flange sign, $325.00.

1940s tin (plate) Whistle sign, $375.00.

1940s embossed tin (plate) screen door "strip" panel, $100.00.

1940s embossed tin sign for Whistle, $300.00.

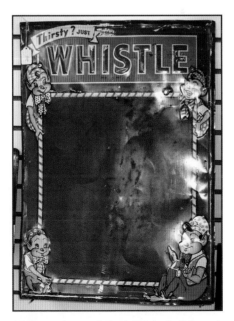

1940s embossed tin (plate) chalkboard,
$160.00.

Spiffy "A Swell Cola Drink" flange sign, $350.00.

Lime Cola bottle cap flange sign, 1950s, $250.00.

Hazle Club Tru-Orange flange sign, $240.00.

"Your Pals Drink Pal Ade", 1950s embossed sign, $175.00.

1950s Ale8 5¢ tin (plate) sign, "It Glorifies", $150.00.

1950s Crescent "Since 1893" tin (plate), $75.00.

Rummy Grapefruit Drink, "A Delicious Beverage," 1950s, $100.00.

Squeeze Orange Drink tin (plate) sign, 1940s, $300.00.

Rochelle Club Beverages sign, embossed, $135.00.

Lemmy Lemonade sign, embossed, 1950s, $160.00.

Wonder Beverages tin (plate) sign, 1950s, $100.00.

Bubble Up tin (plate) sign, embossed, c. late 1950s, $95.00.

Five-O Chocolate embossed sign, 1950s, $130.00. There is an uncon-firmed rumor that Jack Lord loved this drink.

1950s Graf's tin, embossed, especially colorful, $345.00.

Botl'O Orange tin (plate) sign, early 1950s, $130.00.

Nesbitt's Orange sign, 1950s, $140.00.

Brandimist Drink tin (plate) sign, 1940s, $210.00.

Squeeze Drink embossed sign, 1940s, $350.00.

1950s Kist sign, embossed tin (plate), $120.00.

1960s Royal Crown Cola embossed tin (plate) sign, $100.00.

Warwick Club Beverages sign, embossed tin (plate), $140.00.

1930s Monarch revolving sign for orange and root beer, unusual, $500.00.

1940s tin (plate) sign with four different bottles of Bire-ley's displayed, very colorful, $400.00.

Cheer Up sign with seven inserts for different flavors, tin over cardboard, 1950s, $210.00.

Mission Orange Beverages sign. Look closely at this sign because it is a reproduction with no value!

Texas Punch "push" sign for screen door, tin, $125.00.

Nichol Kola sign, tin (plate) with embossed 5¢ bottle, 1936, $180.00.

Big Giant Cola comical bottle sign, embossed tin (plate), 1950s, $200.00.

Squirt embossed chalk-board sign, tin (plate), 1960s, $155.00.

SunCrest tin (plate) sign, embossed bottle, $150.00.

Sweetie Beverages 1950s embossed sign, $145.00.

Door "push" c. 1950s, $100.00.

Pal Ade Drink sign, tin, $125.00.

Korker "Pull" door sign, embossed bottle, $150.00.

Peco Drink "Push" door sign, tin, $135.00.

Mason's Root Beer bottle toper (w/bottle), 1940s – '50s, $55.00.

Frostie door "pull" from the 1950s, $100.00.

Like Diet Drink sign, tin, embossed bottle, 1960s, $160.00.

Bireley's embossed tin (plate), 1940s, $200.00.

Frostie embossed chalkboard tin (plate), 1950s, $140.00.

Royal Crown self-framed sign, 1930s, embossed bottle, tin (plate), $375.00.

Squirt die-cut cardboard, 1960s, $125.00.

Whistle cardboard sign, 1940s, $215.00.

Darrison's die-cut cardboard bottle (5¢), 1940s, $165.00.

Orange-Crush embossed door "push", $200.00.

Green Spot Orange Drink display rack sign, $100.00.

Richardson's Root Beer World's Fair sign, restored, $275.00.

Hires Root Beer barrel dispenser, staved maple with metal bands, c. 1950, $400.00.

Liberty Root Beer dispenser, staved construction, c. 1940s, $375.00.

343

Cherry Smash syrup dispenser, c. 1920s, rare, $2,000.00.

Nesbitt's orange drink sign, celluloid over cardboard, c. 1960, $160.00.

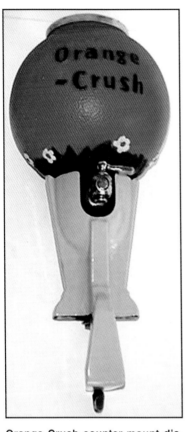

Glass display bottle of Smile soda, $200.00.

Orange Crush counter-mount dispenser, c. 1940, $500.00.

Die-cut bottle of Triple A A A Root Beer, tin (plate) embossed sign, c. 1940s, $375.00.

Tobacciana Containers

Between the American Civil War and the first quarter of the twentieth century there were several thousand different national, regional, and local brands of tobacco products offered for sale. Tax stamps and patent dates can be used to secure an approximate date for any given piece. Keep in mind that a patent number or date indicates that the item was manufactured at some point after the date. If the date is 1902 and the product was in production for 35 years, it could be as late as 1937 but no earlier than 1902.

Among many shapes that the tobacciana products took were the following:

Lunch boxes: rectangular with single or double "drop" or pail handles, similar in form to a wicker or splint picnic basket, but 4" x 6" or less in size and made of tinplate. The lunch box tins began to be marketed after 1900 until about the 1920s.

Store bins: used by the tobaccoist or store keeper for bulk sales. These can be found in ceramic, wood, paper, tinplate, or glass.

"Milk cans" or pails: tinplate canisters with "drop" handle and paper labels, or the milk can with pull-off lid similar in form to the tinplate canister used by school children who packed a lunch and drink for school, the lid resembles a much larger milk container used by dairies. Union Leader is the classic company for manufacturing "milk can" containers.

Figures or figural containers: Mayo, and several other brands, created the Roly-Poly tin shaped like a waiter, Scotland Yard detective, and others about 1912-1918 that encouraged collectors and smokers to buy all five figures.

Pocket tins: containers designed for shirt pockets or back pockets (with a flask-like curve) that held tobacco or "loosies" (cigarettes). There are hundreds of varieties.

Paper packages: the cigarette pack evolved after 1900 with cardboard cards of baseball players, actors, boxers, and bicycle racers used to serve as "stiffeners" for the packaging and to promote the product.

The tobacciana collectibles that follow were sold at Fricker Auctions of LeRoy, Illinois, in the summer of 2005. The price listed with each piece is the "hammer" price.

If You Need A Mission

At a 3rd Sunday Market antiques and collectibles show in October of 1992 (?) in Bloomington, Ill, I came upon two middle-aged men who were in deep and animated discussion. The heavier of the two, in overalls and a John Deere hat, carried a plastic sack in his left hand. I am going to attempt to recreate the dialogue between the two veterans of the hunt.

"Expletive, expletive, I still don't believe it."

"What?"

"I've gone to auctions, shows, markets, and sales for 25 years lookin' for that blue tobacco tin. I got the red and yellow one but I need the blue to complete the set. I've seen it in the books but never in person. Expletive, I got the money, always, it would go for about $1,500.00. but I've never seen one for sale. Expletive."

"I was walkin' down by the drink stand and I saw some guy's booth and from the back he had a blue tin. Right size, right shape, but I've seen a lot before, but never the one. Expletive. He was waitin' on somebody so I waited, My God, it was the blue tin and it was marked $1,295.00. Remember, I got the money and I'd pay the $1,295.00. Quick. Real quick."

I said, "Sir, how much do you need for that tin?"

He picked it up and thought for a minute. He said, "I gotta have $11.00, best I can do."

"I honestly thought I was gonna expletive, expletive expire."

Your mission, should you decide to accept it, is to find a "Ty Cobb Granulated Cut Plug" pocket tin from about 1912. The strong graphic illustrates the left-handed-hitting "Georgia Peach" glaring directly at the buyer, surrounded by a wreath of tobacco. Expect to pay a minimum of $1,000 plus. This tin is an example of a great piece that can take a little more abuse and still maintain significant value.

Box of Frog Cigars with
period cigars, excellent
condition, $200.00.

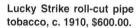

Lucky Strike roll-cut pipe
tobacco, c. 1910, $600.00.

Patterson's Tuxedo Tobacco for pipe & cigarette, unopened, $250.00.

Stag Tobacco jar, $125.00.

Patterson's Tuxedo pipe & cigarette tobacco jar (with contents), $175.00.

Prince Albert jar of prime-cut tobacco, $150.00.

Velvet pipe tocacco in decorative jar, $225.00.

Dill's Best jar of tobacco, $250.00.

Flor De Melba cigars, $100.00.

Tiz cigar tin, $150.00.

Long Distance Chewing or Smoking Tobacco tin, $75.00.

Yum Yum Smoking Tobacco, $100.00.

Sterling Tobacco in counter tin for 5¢ packages, $100.00.

Sweet Mist Chewing Tobacco tin, fine cut, Detroit, Michigan, $125.00.

NiggerHair Smoking Tobacco, $400.00. (This product was changed to BiggerHair in 1927).

Bigger Hair Smoking and Chewing Tobacco counter storage container, $300.00.

Spaulding & Merrick, Landmark, and Reel Smoking Tobacco cannisters, $50.00 (all).

Sweet Mist Chewing Tobacco counter tin, $250.00.

Pedro Smoking Tobacco, $150.00.

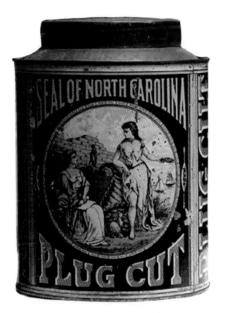

Seal of North Carolina Plug Cut Tobacco tin, $300.00.

Custom House Cigar tin, $125.00.

El Producto Cigar tin, $100.00.

War Eagle Cigars tin, $100.00.

Buster Brown Cigar tin, "2 for 5¢", rare, $3,500.00.

Columbia Cut Plug Smoking Tobacco, made for Sears, Roebuck & Co, $150.00.

Nebraska Blossom tin, $250.00.

Sweet Burley Light Tobacco counter tin, $175.00.

Tiger 5¢ Chewing Tobacco counter tin, $500.00.

Oboid Finest Quality Tobacco,
"No Rubbing Required," $75.00.

Sweet Cuba Light Tobacco counter
tin, $150.00.

Sweet Cuba Dark Tobacco counter
tin, $150.00.

White Seal Tobacco for chewing or
smoking, $125.00.

Black and White Tobacco tin, $225.00.

Sweet Burley Dark Tobacco counter tin, $250.00.

Sun-Kist Smoking Tobacco made for Sears-Roebuck & Co., ripe & mellow, $300.00.

Pure Stock Quality Cigars tin, (5¢), $75.00.

Gobblers Tobacco tin, $300.00.

Sterling Dark Tobacco counter tin, $275.00.

Just Suits Cut Plug Tobacco in "lunch-box" tin, $50.00.

Penny Post Tobacco in "lunchbox", $75.00.

Rose Leaf Chewing Tobacco counter container, $300.00.

Dan Patch Cut Plug tin. This tin was part of a "warehouse find" in about 1970 and was offered for $5.00 – 10.00 at that time, $75.00.

George Washington Tobacco in "lunchbox", $75.00.

Sweet Cuba Chewing Tobacco bucket, paper label, "drop" handle, c. 1912, $500.00.

Mayo's Cut Plug Tobacco, "lunchbox," $100.00.

Patterson's Tuxedo Tobacco, for smoking or pipes, $150.00.

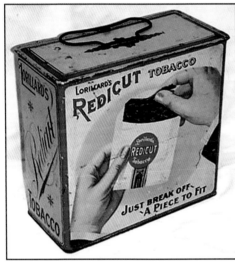

Redicut Tobacco "lunchbox" tin, "Just Break Off A Piece To Fit." $175.00.

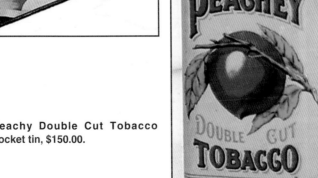

Peachy Double Cut Tobacco pocket tin, $150.00.

Autobacco Pipe Tobacco tin, c. 1908, $150.00.

Sure Shot Chewing Tobacco counter tin, porcelain pull, (rare), $1,200.00.

Game counter tin, contained 48 nickel packs, fine cut, $700.00.

Mail Pouch Chewing Tobacco counter tin, $350.00.

Sweet Cuba Fine Cut Tobacco counter display tin,
contained four dozen 5¢ packages, $200.00.

Sweet Cuba display tin, "Always Fresh, Just as it Left the
Factory," $500.00.

Polar Bear Tobacco display bin, rare form, $1,500.00.

Red Band Scrap Tobacco tin, "Always-Fresh." $1,000.00.

Dixie Kid Cut Plug Tobacco "lunchbox" tin, $400.00.

Union Leader Cut Plug Tobacco container, cardboard stock, $400.00.

Buckingham Cut Plug Smoking Tobacco pocket tin, $125.00.

Sweet Mist Chewing Tobacco counter display, $250.00.

Tiger Tobacco, 5¢ packages, counter display, $250.00.

King Midas Handmade Cigars tin, $200.00.

Big Ben Smoking Tobacco pocket tin, $50.00.

Stag Tobacco tins for pipe and cigarettes, $475.00 (pair).

Sunset Trail Cigars tin, 5¢ each, $400.00.

Miners & Puddlers
Smoking Tobacco,
$50.00.

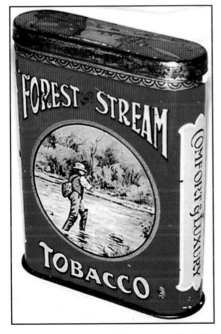

Forest and Stream Tobacco pocket tin,
$275.00.

Red Jacket pocket tin, $125.00.

Central Union Tobacco, pocket tin, $200.00.

Forest and Stream Pipe Tobacco
pocket tin, $100.00.

Hi-Plane Tobacco pocket tins, $175.00 (pair).

Honey Moon Tobacco pocket tin, $150.00.

City Club Tobacco pocket tin, crushed cubes, $350.00.

Pick (Burley) Tobacco tin, $100.00.

Stag Tobacco pocket tin, $100.00.

Three Feathers Plug Cut
Tobacco pocket tin, $400.00.

Times Square Smoking Mixture
pocket tin, c. 1925, $400.00.

Puritan Crushed Plug Mixture, pocket tin, $250.00.

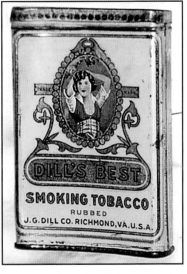

Dill's Best Smoking Tobacco pocket tin, $125.00.

Pipe Major English Smoking Mixture pocket tin, $300.00.

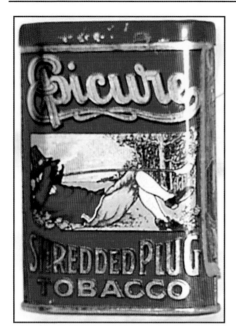

Epicure Shredded Plug Tobacco pocket tin, $225.00.

Condition is critical to the value of any collectible, but the degree of rarity allows some examples to take "bigger hits" than others. This tin, in exceptional condition, is worth about $75.00 – 80.00. The much rarer Bull Dog pocket tin sold for $500.00 in a considerably lesser condition.

Bagley's Old Colony Mixture Smoking Tobacco pocket tin, unopened, $375.00.

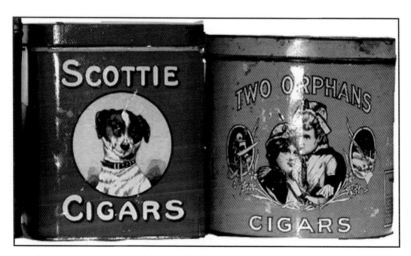

Scottie Cigars and Two Orphans Cigars tins, Scottie $300.00; Two Orphans, $200.00.

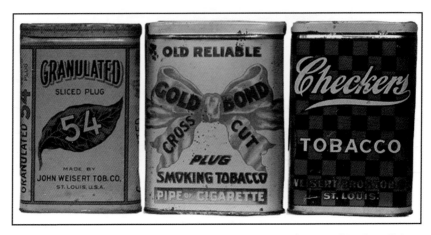

54 pocket tin, $200.00; Gold Bond Old Reliable Tobacco, $250.00; Checkers Tobacco pocket tin, $400.00.

Bowl of Roses pocket tin, $200.00; Lucky Strike Tobacco pocket tin, $150.00; Full Dress Tobacco pocket tin, $175.00.

Tropics cigar box, c. 1912, $100.00.

G.C. Rutter's cigar box, $75.00.

Caballero cigar box, $75.00.

Continental cigar box, $75.00.

Eyerly Bros' Speed King cigar box, c. 1910, $200.00.

Speckled Pups cigar box, $100.00.

Moki cigar box, $75.00.

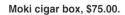

Old North Bridge cigar box, $75.00.

Key West Florida District "Temptation" cigar box, $125.00.

Golden Pheasant (10¢) cigar box, $75.00.

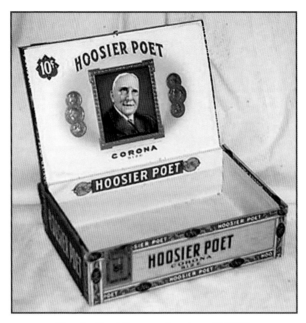

Hoosier Poet Corona cigar box, $175.00.

Town Talk cigar box, $75.00.

Geo's Favorite cigar box, "A Sure Winner," $75.00.

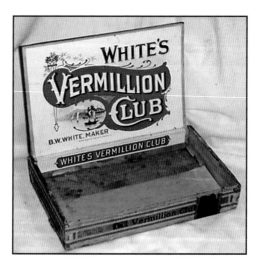

White's Vermillion Club cigar box, $75.00.

War Eagle Cheroots cigar box, "three for 5¢", $150.00.

Tree Cutter cigar box, $100.00.

Betsy Ross 5¢ cigar box, $150.00.

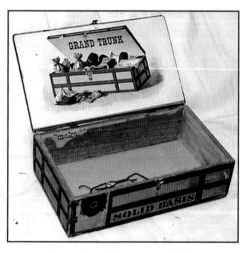

Grand Trunk cigar box, $75.00.

Warsaw Eagle cigar box, $75.00.

Hank Rice cigar box, $75.00.

Night Hawk cigar box, $75.00.

Chas. P. Stanley Treaty Bond cigar box,
$75.00.

Duquesne Club 6¢ cigar box, $75.00.

Buffalo N.Y. Sweet Moments cigar box, $75.00.

Pony Post cigar box, $75.00.

Smoker Etto cigar box, $100.00.

Big Feather cigar box, $100.00.

C.H. Brenaman & Co. cigar box, $100.00.

Cannon Ball cigar box, $125.00.

Kewanee cigar box, $100.00.

Washtella (5¢) cigar box, $75.00.

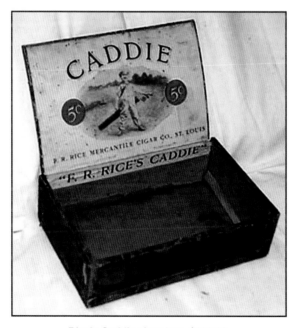

Rice's Caddie cigar box, $150.00.

Camp Fire "2 for 5¢" cigar box, $75.00.

Chief Pontiac cigar box from Milton Junction, WI, $75.00.

White Indian "Handmade 5¢ Cigar" box,
$75.00.

Young Chief cigar box, $100.00.

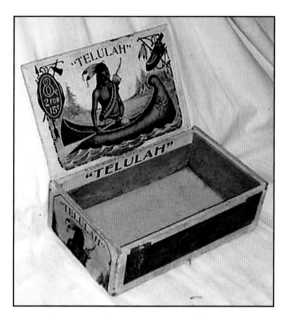

Telulah "2 for 15¢" cigar box, $100.00.

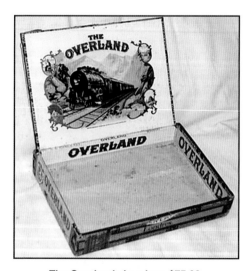

The Overland cigar box, $75.00.

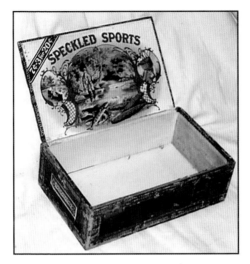

Speckled Sports "7¢ – 3 for 20¢", $75.00.

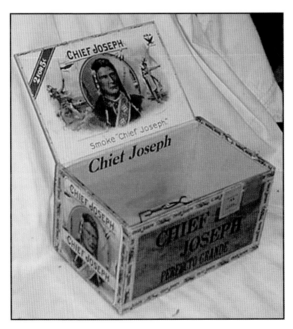

Chief Joseph "2 for 5¢" cigars, $100.00.

La Indiana cigar box, $75.00.

Our Game cigar box, $100.00.

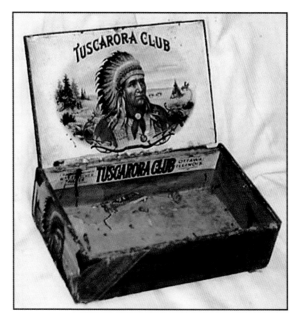

Tuscarora Club, $100.00.

Royal Princess "handmade" cigar box, $100.00.

TR (Theodore Roosevelt) "Invincibles" cigar box, c. 1912, $125.00.

Montana Sport Carrier Cigar Co. cigar box, $75.00.

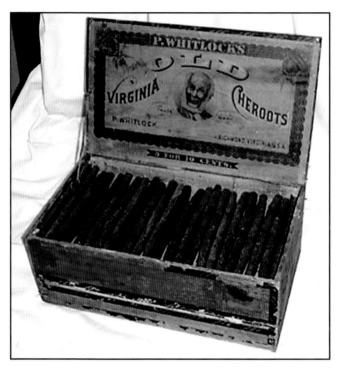

P. Whitlock's Old Virginia Cheroots cigar box (full), $250.00.

Old Virginia Cheroots cigar box with drop
front, $50.00.

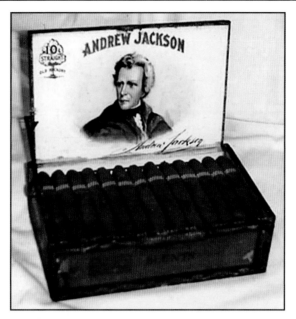

Andrew Jackson cigar box with contents, $100.00.

Black Ben "3 for 5¢" cigar box, $150.00.

Pittsburg Smoke cigar box, $125.00.

Fifty-Fifty cigars and box, $125.00.

Fire Brigade cigar box, $300.00.

Coon Skin cigar box, $200.00; Lutz's Frog cigar box, $100.00.

Box of Brown's Mule Chewing Tobacco, $50.00.

Assorted packages of tobacco: Whale-back, King Bird, Pick, & Honey Moon, in "rough" condition, $150.00 (all).

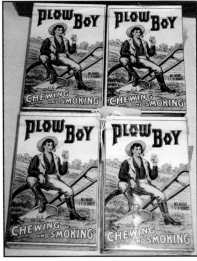

Plow Boy Chewing and Smoking Tobacco, $50.00 (all).

"Bull" Durham pocket pouches, box of ten, $175.00.

Carton of Tiger Cigarettes, $100.00.

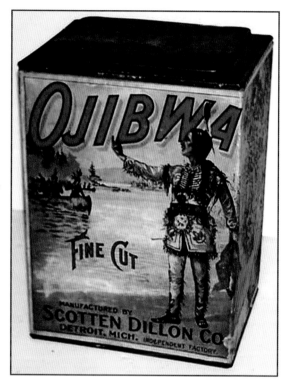

Ojibwa counter box, $800.00.

Country Gentlemen box for 5¢ bags, $500.00.

405

Drum Smoking Tobacco box, $500.00.

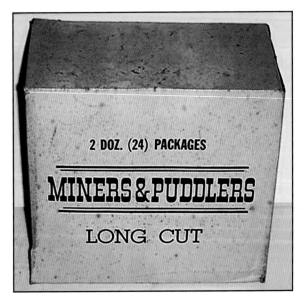

Miners & Pubblers Long Cut Tobacco, full box, $400.00.

Bagley's Sweet Tips pocket tins, box of 12, $200.00.

Blue Moon Union Made Tocacco, contains individual packages of tobacco, $1,200.00.

Buffalo Smoking Tobacco box with individual pouches
of tobacco, $275.00.

Lucky Strike Cigarettes, box of 12, $200.00.

Double-Mellow Old Gold Cigarettes, $200.00.

Old Gold Cigarettes box, $125.00.

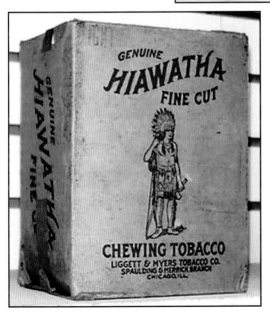

Hiawatha Chewing Tobacco box, $300.00.

Peachey Chewing Tobacco, box of 12, $100.00.

Kentucky's Best Smoking Tobacco, in bag, $75.00.

Handsome Dan Mixture, box sports "Yale Mascot" logo, $150.00.

Snow Flake Smoking Tobacco, 10¢, $75.00.

Pay Car Scrap Tobacco pack, $150.00.

Veteran Tobacco pack, $50.00.

Red Man Chewing Tobacco banner, $75.00.

Sure Shot Chewing Tobacco, "It Touches the Spot", $125.00.

Homerun Cigarettes, unopened pack, $75.00.

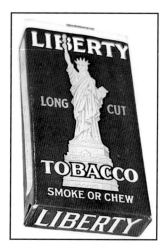

Liberty Tobacco, $50.00.

4 Bagger Tobacco, $125.00.

Sour Apple Tobacco, King Bird Tobacco, & Summer-time Tobacco, $50.00 (all).

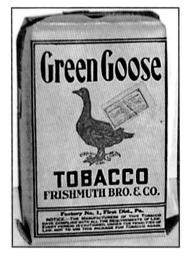

Box of Green Goose Tobacco, $100.00.

Bleidersdorf & Co., bag (pouch) of pipe tobacco, $75.00.

Bowl of Roses Pipe Tobacco Mixture, Oceanic Cut Plug Tobacco, $50.00 (both).

413

Giant Tobacco, $125.00; Drummer Boy, $50.00; Pep Cigarettes, $50.00.

Black Rose Cigar Clippings, $50.00; La Turka Tobacco, $50.00.

Rob Roy Pipe Tobacco, $100.00 (both).

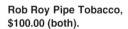

King Bird Smoking Tobacco, $100.00 (both).

Summer-time Long Cut Tobacco, $75.00 (both).

Uncle Daniel Fine Cut Tobacco, unopened, $50.00.

Honest Smoking and Chewing Tobacco, $100.00.

Bull Dog Tobacco, single-sided tin (metal) flange sign, $800.00.

La Turka Cigarettes, $75.00.

Whale Smoking Tobacco, $100.00.

Greenback Smoking Tobacco, $500.00.

"Call for Philip Morris" die-cut stand-up, c. 1050, $175.00.

Bob White Granulated Smoking Tobacco, $500.00.

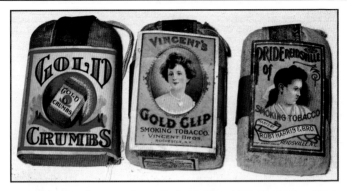

Gold Crumbs, $75.00; Vincent's Gold Clip, $125.00; Pride of Reidsville, $100.00.

King Alfred Cigar sign, $500.00.

Chesterfield counter display, with pipe, $400.00.

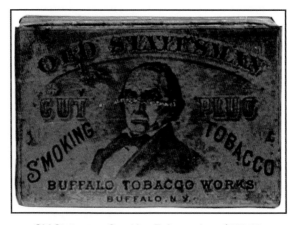

Old Statesman Smoking Tobacco box, $150.00.

Plaster-of-paris (chalk) counter display of Native American warrior, $225.00.

Indian Chief plaster-of-paris (chalk) counter display, c. 1920, $350.00.

Velvet Tobacco container, ornate type sold at Christmas, $125.00.

420

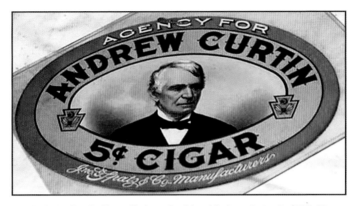

Andrew Curtin "hang" sign, double-sided card stock, $150.00.

Pippins cigar package, 5¢ cigars, $275.00.

Silas, Peirce & Co's 1815 "10 cent cigar" sign, $75.00.

Castle Hall Cigars sign, hangs from the beak of a paper mache stork in store display, package of two, $150.00.

Odin 5¢ Cigar paper broadside, $500.00.

Camels (sst) metal sign, c. 1950, $75.00.

William Fredrick's 5¢ cigar pennant & Fredrick's cigar tin, $300.00.

SpearHead Chewing Tobacco metal sign (sst), $400.00.

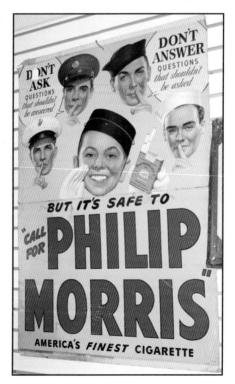

WW II Philip Morris paper broadside, c. 1943, $200.00.

#98 racer from Japan, $1,800.00.

#8 Indianapolis 500 racer (Japan), $700.00.

Marx #5 racer (U.S.), $125.00.

#42 Super Racer (French), $1,500.00.

Early 1930s Indianapolis Motor Speedway pennant, silk screened, $200.00.

Marx #7 racer (U.S.), $125.00.

Marx #3 racer (U.S.), $125.00.

Marx #5 racer (U.S.) veteran of hundreds of races, $50.00.

#5 racer (Japan), $100.00.

Strauss #7 tin (plate) racer, $225.00.

Thimble Drome #35 racer, $250.00.

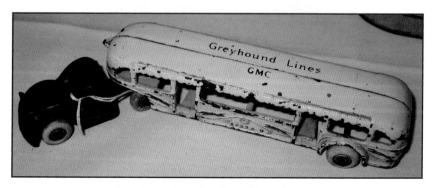

Arcade cast iron Greyhound bus, $225.00.

Thimble Drome racer, #16, $250.00.

Ohlsson & Rice #42, racer with box, $600.00.

Thimble Drome racer with driver, #2, $300.00.

Thimble Drome #51 racer with box, $4,400.00.

Thimble Drome #25 racer, $250.00.

1950s Buddy L dump truck, $75.00.

Small cast iron "stake" truck, worn surface, $75.00.

Marx climbing tractor with driver and box, $500.00.

Hercules dump truck, $225.00.

Buddy L dump truck, $900.00.

Buddy L truck, $1,000.00.

Wyandotte tin (plate) car, $150.00.

Arcade, cast iron, with driver, $300.00.

Rapid Express dump truck, $75.00.

Cast-iron Arcade Mack truck (restored), $750.00.

Hoge car, $300.00.

Cast-iron car, $100.00.

Hoge fire-chief car with original tag, $375.00.

Cast-iron convertible, $125.00.

Marx yellow cab wind-up, $150.00.

Strauss #21 racer, $350.00.

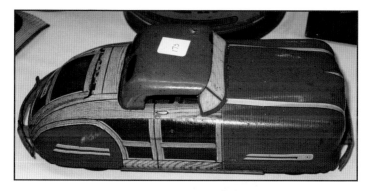

Tin friction car, 1940s, $150.00.

Marx Speed King racer, $450.00.

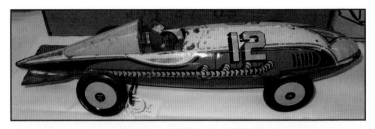

Tin windup #12 racer, $175.00.

Rocket Racer, tin (plate) wind-up, $175.00.

#5 plastic wind-up racer, $75.00.

Golden Jet #18 racer, $125.00.

Thimble Drome #3 racer, $275.00.

The Race Master #8 racer, $125.00.

Thimble Drome #12, $250.00.

439

Thimble Drome #28 racer with box, $400.00.

Thimble Drome racer #51, $275.00.

Thimble Drome #7 racer, $250.00.

#93 Thimble Drome racer, $250.00.

Absentee bid: a written offer, left in advance, for an item to be auctioned. The bidder will not physically be at the auction but his bid for a specific item will be present. The absentee bid sets the limit of his bid. If it sells for less than his offer, he wins it at that price.

Absolute auction: an auction where the highest bid takes the item. If an item is at "absolute" auction there is no reserve or minimum bid. Absolute auctions are considerably more rare than auctions with some form of reserve.

Admission: admission is rarely, if ever, charged for getting into an auction. In situations where the items offered at auction were owned by movie stars, the Kennedy family, etc. there could be an admission by catalog which would require the advance purchase of the catalog to control the size of the crowd.

As it is, where it is: a standard term that indicates there are no guarantees and the successful bidder must remove the item from the premises. The buyer is buying on "his own knowledge."

Buy-in (bought-in): an item that is bought-in is sold to a bidder's number that is represented by the auctioneer or the seller of the goods. For example, #32 belongs to a bidder who is buying for the "house" because an item did not meet the minimum "reserve" determined by the owner. According to the Uniform Commercial Code adopted by 49 states, this process is certainly unethical and probably illegal in most jurisdictions.

Buyer's premium: a toll or fee paid by the buyer (often 12 – 20%) that goes to the auctioneer to help defray expenses.

Buyer's remorse: an emotional and negative response by the buyer after he/she bids successfully and then realizes that too much was paid.

Choice: if a box contains four cast iron doorstops offered as a single lot and the auctioneer says "Choice" the successful bidder (who won with a $100.00 bid) can take the one he wants for $100.00 or all four for $400.00 (same money). If he passes, others in the audience can have the same opportunity.

Christie's (christie's.com): one of three or four upscale American auction houses that operate on an international basis.

Closing out sale: an auction of parts, machines, vehicles, household goods, tools (often farm related) when a farmer or small business ceases to continue. (Often held "on-site").

Condition of sale: the general terms under which an item is sold at auction. The aforementioned "as it is, where it is" is the basis for condition of sale.

Consignor: the owner(s) of the items to be offered for sale at the auction.

Eclectic collector's auction: a relatively new term that refers to a wide variety of junk, antiques, and collectibles brought together at auction by a collector of a myriad of catagories

Ephemera: generally paper goods that could consist of catalogs, road maps, advertisements, handbills, newspapers, or broadsides produced for short term use but saved for some reason by the collector

Estate auction: following a death the owner's heirs relegate his holdings for sale at auction. Often, of course, the heirs have picked and chosen some of the deceased's possessions to stay within the bounds of the family and /or friends.

Fees: an attempt by the consignor to negotiate the percentage taken by the auctioneer, photography expenses, moving the items, advertising the auction, catalog expenses, and a charge for items that don't meet the reserve and are returned to the consignor. The number of "rings," runners, and ring men could also be part of the discussion in some instances.

Floor: usually refers to the audience at the auction as in "sold to the floor" rather than to a telephone bid or a left bid.

Gaffed auction: an auction where some of the offerings are fakes/reproductions and are knowingly being offered for sale hidden among legitimate merchandise. This is a major step beyond "salting."

Hammer price: the actual selling price of the item at auction. The buyer's premium is typically added to, and is a percentage of, the "hammer" price.

Jump-bid: an adventurous technique used by a bidder to take a bid from $300.00 to $500.00 when the auctioneer is looking for $25.00 increments.

Left bid: comparable to an absentee bid. Used by a bidder who will not physically be at the auction but who has left a bid to be placed for him by a member of the auctioneer's staff. This limits how high the potential buyer will bid and secures the piece for him at less than his bid if it is the highest. For example, the left bid is $475.00 and the item sells for $325.00. The left bid buys the item for $325.00 (plus a buyer's premium if applicable).

Number: the card or paddle with a printed number that is given to the potential bidder when he/she registers. All sales won wil be charged to that bidder's account number. Usually calls for identification and a specific letter of credit at serious (very serious) auctions.

"No sale": a term used by the auctioneer when the reserve for a specific item is not met or reached.

Pre-estate auction: a couple (or individual) disposes of many of his/her/their possessions prior to death and prior to making major changes in lifestyle.

On-site: ususally refers to the auction taking place at the seller's home or business location and not in the facilities of the auctioneer.

On-the-phone: a bidder who is monitoring the sale of the item he desires and is bidding for it over the telephone. The "on-the-phone" bidder is in competition with the floor and any "left" bids.

On your own knowledge: your only guarantee is your own awareness of understanding of what a particular item is. The consignor and auctioneer offer nothing other than the item.

Phantom bid: a technique used when an auctioneer accepts a bid from a number without a human attached to it. This is typically done when the reserve is not reached or the auctioneer is not pleased with the amount bid to that point. If the phantom bid does not rally the floor, the phantom may purchase the item.

Pool: another unethical and illegal act in most jurisdictions used to keep hammer prices depresssed. Rather than compete against each other, a group of bidders agrees not to bid against one another. The items purchased by the "pool" are then auctioned off among themselves after the auction is concluded.

Presale estimate: an amount that is a "fair market" estimate of the value of a piece prior to the auction and appears next to the item's picture in a catalog. Often the presale estimate is more conservative than "fair market" value. We recently saw a $1,000.00 bill offered with a presale estimate of $400.00.

Preview: a pre-sale exhibit or opportunity to see the items upclose prior to the actual auction. Could be several hours or a few days before the auction.

Principal: the individual(s) offering the goods for sale, the owner.

Reserve: the amount established by the consignor (seller) that he/she must have before the item can be sold at auction. If the reserve is too high, it may not be met and the piece is not sold.

Rings: at farm sales, there is often so much merchandise to sell that two or three auctions are taking place simultaneously in the same venue.

Ring man: an assistant who helps conduct the sale by holding up the item in one of the selling rings or on the floor.

Runner: an individucal who works for the auctioneer and assists in the selling process much like a ring man. Could physically hold up merchandise so the floor can see or help in "spotting" bids in many instances.

Salting: another unethical practice that is growing in some areas. An example is when a prominent collector dies and the auctioneer brings in merchandise from other sources to sell with the possessions of the deceased. The audience assumes that all goods being offered are from the same collection. The "salted" items are usually of a lesser quality than the items heavily advertised and often come in through the back door.

Shill: an individual planted on the floor to raise bids for an item by appearing to be a bidder but in reality is an employee of the auctioneer or consignor. The word is shortened from "shilliber."

Sotheby's: (sotheby's.com) another of three to four national auction houses with international business and reputation.

Speciality auction: an auction devoted to a single category of items. Examples could range from stamps to wine. Usually happens when a collection of carnival glass or other category is offered from one source or an estate. The bidders can be fewer in number but very serious.

Uniform Commercial Code: business code established currently in 49 states that regulates transactions. Established in the early 1950s. Has serious effects on the operation of auction houses and transactions. Most consumers are unfamiliar with the UCC.

Withdrawn: an item that is removed from the auction. Could be caused by new information or the failure to meet a reserve.

Bonus to the Lexicore Reader

You have been so attentive that we are going to toss in "Fair market value."

Fair market value is establied when a buyer and seller reach an agreement on a price. Both parties are under *no* pressure to buy or to sell and are engaging in the dialogue voluntarily (because they want to) not because they "have" to.

Read each question carefully. The statement is either True or False. There is no other alternative.

1. T or F — There are more "absolute" auctions each year than "reserved" auctions.

2. T or F — If the auction advertisement doesn't state to the contrary, you can assume it is an "absolute" auction.

3. T or F — If you make a purchase at a typical auction, you have 5 business days to return the item if you are not pleased with it.

4. T or F — The hammer price is the opening price asked for by the auctioneer.

5. T or F — Salting occurs when items are removed from the estate by relatives or heirs prior to the estate auction.

6. T or F — Ephemera could include telephone books and junk mail from 1934.

7. T or F — A shill can be used by the auctioneer to enhance the bidding.

8. T or F — A "pool" must consist of a minimum of one potential buyer.

9. T or F — The national standard for a buyer's premium is 5%.

10. T or F — The buyer usually has a minimum of 48 hours to remove his purchase from the auction site.

The answers can be found at the bottom of this page.

Bonus question: What is the official soft drink of Maine?

Answers: All statements are false with the exceptions of 6 & 7

Bonus question answer: Moxie

Raycrafts' Americana Price Guide

Volume One
Don & R.C. Raycraft

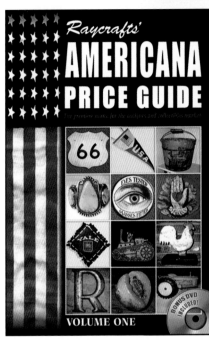

This price guide is the premier source for information on what to look for, how to make sure it's real, and up-to-date values for a wide range of collectibles that are still available at markets, antique shows, garage sales, estate auctions, and Internet auctions. Covering a little bit of everything and housing more than 950 color photos, the book and DVD contain information on Depression glass, Boy Scouts Memorabilia, advertising, Marx and Schoenhut toys, golf clubs, fishing lures, jewelry, postcards, cookie jars, coffee mills, pennants, and more. 2006 values.

Item #6842 • ISBN: 1-57432-481-0
5½ x 8½ • 352 Pgs. • PB • $19.95

The DVD features professional dealers who share their insights and secrets on collecting. The Raycrafts bring years of antiques and collectibles experience to the pages of this handy, must-have collector's resource. 2006 values.

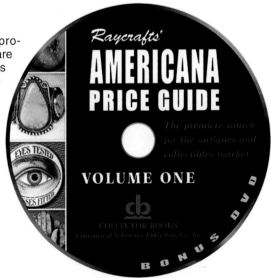

Schroeder's ANTIQUES Price Guide

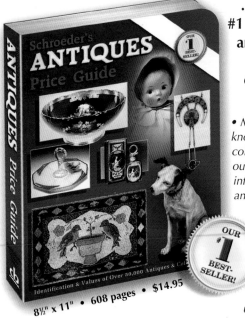

**...is the
#1 bestselling
antiques & collectibles
value guide
on the market today,
and here's why...**

• More than 400 advisors, well-known dealers, and top-notch collectors work together with our editors to bring you accurate information regarding pricing and identification.

• More than 50,000 items in over 500 categories are listed along with hundreds of sharp original photos that illustrate not only the rare and unusual, but the common, popular collectibles as well.

8½" x 11" • 608 pages • $14.95

• Each large close-up shot shows important details clearly. Every subject is represented with histories and background information, a feature not found in any of our competitors' publications.

• Our editors keep abreast of newly developing trends, often adding several new categories a year as the need arises.

**Without doubt, you'll find
*Schroeder's Antiques
Price Guide*
the only one to buy for reliable
information and values.**

COLLECTOR BOOKS
P.O. Box 3009
Paducah, KY 42002–3009
www.collectorbooks.com